1006
SALT & PEPPER SHAKERS: ADVERTISING

Larry Carey & Sylvia Tompkins

Schiffer Publishing Ltd

4880 Lower Valley Road, Atglen, PA 19310 USA

ACKNOWLEDGMENTS

We greatly appreciate the encouragement and assistance of fellow collectors, and especially the following contributors to this book:

Quent Christman, Barbara Cummings, Nigel Dalley, Ann Ebner, Dot Gammon, Bob Gentile, Shirley Gimondo, Joan Green, Judy Hankins, Betty & Freddie Hunter, Wendy Johnston, Heath Karr, Ralph & Sharon Karr, Mike Kaul, Jeanne Langer, Donna Leiby, Susan Lerner, Eric Lodge, Phil Mays, Myrna Meyer, Jean Moon, Joanne Rose, Carolyn Schaffer, John Sirbaugh, Josephine & Walt Stanish, Irene Thornburg, Dorothy Troxtell, Marjorie Watson

Our special thanks to Marty Grossman and Peter Capell, whose assistance with this book has been very valuable.

Copyright © 2000 by Larry Carey and Sylvia Tompkins
Library of Congress Card Number: 00-101062

Book design by "Sue"
Type set in Lithograph/Zurich Bt

ISBN: 0-7643-1185-9
Printed in China
1 2 3 4

Published by Schiffer Publishing Ltd.
4880 Lower Valley Road
Atglen, PA 19310
Phone: (610) 593-1777; Fax: (610) 593-2002
E-mail: Schifferbk@aol.com
Please visit our web site catalog at
www.schifferbooks.com or write for a free catalog.

We are always looking for authors to write books on new and related subjects. If you have an idea for a book, please contact us at the above address.

This book may be purchased from the publisher.
Please include $3.95 for shipping.

In Europe, Schiffer books are distributed by
Bushwood Books
6 Marksbury Ave.
Kew Gardens
Surrey TW9 4JF England
Phone: 44 (0)208 392-8585; Fax: 44 (0)208 392-9876
E-mail: Bushwd@aol.com
Free postage in the UK. Europe: Air mail at cost.
Please try your bookstore first.

CONTENTS

INTRODUCTION

Although advertising sets represent only one category of salt and pepper shakers, they offer a wide variety of subjects to attract many collectors. Ranging in size from the half-inch airline shakers to soda or pop bottles standing over six inches tall, these sets are made of cardboard, plastic, ceramic, metal, glass, wood, and combinations thereof. Almost every S&P collection includes at least one advertising set; many collectors specialize in this area, or a portion of it, like gas pumps.

A question arises about the difference between advertising and souvenirs. In some instances, the line is very fine. We are portraying advertising as sets that represent a product or service. Services include transportation, retail establishments, and entertainment, such as television shows, movies and sports teams. Souvenir sets are primarily from a tourist attraction such as the Eiffel Tower in Paris, the Statue of Liberty in New York, and Disneyworld in Florida, so they are not included. However, we agree a case can be made either way! There was not enough room to include all the beverage S&Ps we had, so we were not about to search for additional sets!

In the past year, internet auctions have had a significant effect on S&P prices. While some top of the line sets have seen price increases, the reverse has been true in many areas. This trend is reflected in the prices shown, which are based on experience plus input from these auctions and contributors. As always, values are intended only as a guide and will vary based on condition, geographical area, knowledge of the seller or buyer, number of interested parties, and sometimes just luck. Sets are ceramic unless noted otherwise.

THE NOVELTY SALT & PEPPER SHAKERS CLUB

The Novelty Salt and Pepper Shakers Club is an international organization of 1,400 members. These collectors enjoy friendships and benefits derived from joining with others who share a love of their hobby. Twenty-one regional chapters (eighteen American and three Canadian) afford an opportunity for collectors to get together with others in their area. Each year the Club's convention is held in a different part of the country to give as many members as possible a chance to attend. Quarterly newsletters provide information on shaker identification and history, as well as a means to buy, sell and trade. For more information about the Club, please contact the authors.

TRANSPORTATION

AIRLINES

Sizes range from .5 to 2". Country of origin is same as country of airline, or unknown, unless stated.

Aeroflot (Russia). 1980s. $35-40.

Air Canada. 1990s. Plastic. $6-8.

Air Canada. Taiwan, 1980s. Glass. $8-10.

Air Canada. Regina '83 Silver Broom. 3.5". 1980s. $12-15.

Air Canada. 1990s. Plastic. $6-8.

Two sets from Air Canada. England, 1990s. Royal Doulton. $20-22.

Air Afrique (Cote d'Ivoire-Ivory Coast). 1990s. Plastic. $12-15.

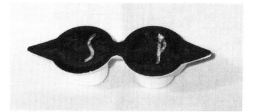

Air France. 1980s. $10-12.

Air France. 1980s. Plastic with metal tops. $10-12.

Air France. 1970s. Metal. $12-15.

Air Liberte (France). Plastic. $15-18.

Air France. Left set, 1970s, plastic. $10-12. Right set, 1990s, Concorde, ceramic. $15-18.

Left:
Air India. 1970s.
Plastic. $18-20.

AOM (Air Outre Mer, France). England. 1960s. $20-25.

Left:
Air Zimbabwe.
England, 1990s.
Wedgwood. $22-25.

Air Pacific (Fiji). Japan, 1990s. Noritake. $25-30

Air New Zealand. 1980s. Left set, Japan, Noritake. $15-18. Right set, Crown Lynn Potteries, New Zealand. $20-22.

Right:
Alia, Royal Jordanian Airline. Japan, 1990s. $25-30.

Alitalia (Aerolinee Italiane Internazionali, Italy). 1990s. EMP Roma. Plastic. $15-18

Air New Zealand. Probably Japan, 1960s. Plastic. $10-12.

America West Airlines. Taiwan, 1980s. Glass with metal tops. $10-12.

Allegheny Airlines (USA). 1950s. Plastic. $22-25.

Asiana (South Korea). 1990s. Bone china S&P, plastic tray. $25-30.

ANA (Australian National Airline). 1960s. Plastic. Merged with Ansett Australia. $25-28.

American Airlines. Left set, 1950s, cardboard, $20-22. Right set, 1980s, plastic, $8-10.

American. 4.25". 1950s. Originally filled with cocktails or liquor. Glass with plastic tops. $10-12.

C & S. (USA). 1950s. Plastic. Probably an early regional airline that merged with Delta. $25-30.

American. Left set, metal, 1960s, $22-25. Right set, Taiwan, 1990s, glass with metal tops, $10-12.

Braniff International Airways (USA). 1960s. Plastic. $12-15.

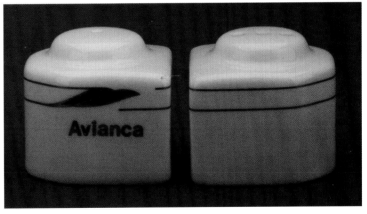

Avianca (Columbia). Japan, 1960s. $30-35.

Braniff. 1950s. Plastic. $12-15.

British Airways. 1980s.
Royal Doulton. $22-25.

British Airways. 1990s. Left set, Concorde, Royal Doulton.
Right set, Wedgwood. $25-30.

Belgian World Airways. 1950s. One-piece
plastic set, two sets shown. $20-22.

British Airways. 1970s. Plastic. $10-12.

BOAC (British Overseas Airways). Left set, Ridgeway, 1970s,
$15-18. Right sets, 1950s, plastic. $22-25.

Left:
BEA (British European Airways).
1950s. Plastic. $15-18.

Right:
British Airways. Left set, 1990s,
plastic, $8-10. Right set, 1950s,
cardboard, $12-15. Top set,
1980s, Royal Doulton, $15-18.

British Caledonian Airways. 1990s. Royal Doulton. $20-22.

BEA. 1950s. Left set, one-piece cardboard and metal. Top set, cardboard and metal. Center and right sets, plastic. $22-25.

CP Air (Canadian Pacific, now part of Canadian Airlines), 1970s. Right set is plastic. $10-12.

Left:
Canada 3000. China, 1990s. Plastic. $6-8.

China Airlines (Republic of China). 1990s. $22-25.

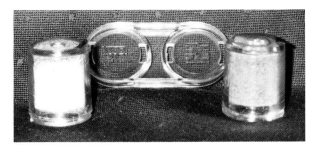

Canadian Pacific Air Lines. China, 1990s. Plastic. $8-10.

Canadian Airlines International. Taiwan, 1980s. Glass with metal tops. $8-10.

Cathay Pacific Airways (Hong Kong). Japan, 1990s. Noritake. $25-30.

Cathay Pacific. 1990s. Glass with plastic tops. $10-12.

Cathay Pacific. Japan, 1990s. $15-18.

Cathay Pacific. Japan, 1990s. $18-20.

Continental Airlines (USA). 1950s. Plastic. $12-15.

Cathay Pacific. England, 1950s. Plastic. $12-15.

Left and above:
Continental. Taiwan, 1980s. Glass with metal tops. $10-12.

Delta Air Lines (USA).
1950s. Plastic. $15-18.

Delta. 1980s. $22-25.

Eastern Air Lines (USA). 1950s.
Plastic. $18-20.

Egypt Air. 1990s. $22-25.

Eastern. Taiwan. 1970s. Left set, ceramic. Right set, glass with metal tops. $18-20.

Egypt Air. 1990s. Metal.
$20-22.

Frontier Airlines (USA).
1950s. Cardboard. $15-18.

Egypt Air. England. 1990s. $20-22.

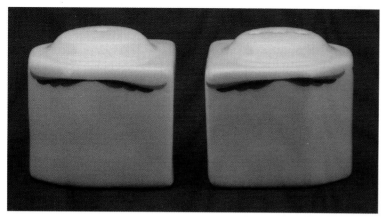

EVA Air (Taiwan). Japan, 1960s. Noritake. $25-30.

Finnair (Finland). 1980s. Plastic. $12-15.

Ghana Airways. England, 1960s.
Plastic. $20-22.

Finnair. 1980s. Plastic. $12-15.

Gulf Air (Bahrain). England, 1990s.
Wedgwood Hotelware. $25-30.

Gulf Air. Japan, 1990s. Noritake.
$25-30.

Gulf Air. 1990s. $25-30

Right:
Iberia Airlines (Spain). 1980s.
Guillen, Madrid. $20-22.

JAL. 1970s. Plastic. $12-15.

Japan Airlines (JAL). 1980s. Glass with
metal tops on plastic tray. $10-12.

Right:
JAT—Yugoslav
Airlines. 1980s.
$20-22.

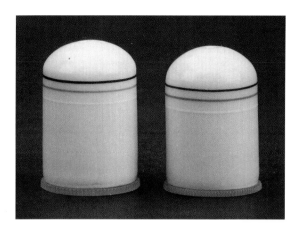

KLM—Royal Dutch Airlines. Japan, 1980s. $20-22.

KLM. 1950s. Wooden shoe with plastic shakers. $12-15.

KLM. 1950s. Plastic. $12-15.

KLM. 1980s. Glass with metal tops. $8-10.

Korean Air. 1980s. Glass with metal tops on plastic tray. $10-12.

Kuwait Airways. Taiwan, 1980s. Glass with metal tops. $12-15.

Kuwait Airways. Japan, 1990s. Narumi. $25-30.

Lauda Air (Austria). 1990s. $15-18.

LOT Polish Airlines. 1950s. One-piece plastic set. $15-18.

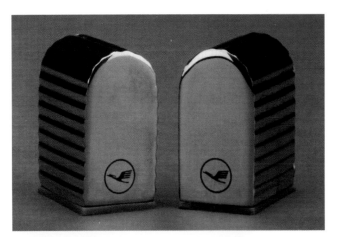

Lufthansa German Airlines. 1970s. Metal. $20-22.

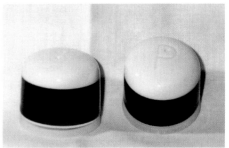

Lufthansa. 1990s. $15-18.

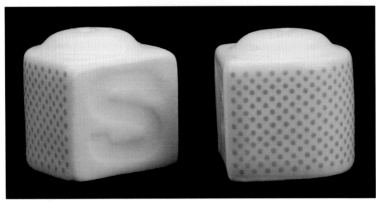

Left:
Lufthansa. 1980s. $22-25.

Right:
Lufthansa. 1950s. One-piece plastic set. $15-18.

Midwest Express Airlines (USA). Japan, 1980s. Glass with metal tops. $12-15.

Middle East Airlines SA (Lebanon). England, 1990s. Royal Doulton. $30-35.

Nigeria Airways. England, 1990s. Royal Doulton. $30-35.

Pan Am. Taiwan, 1980s. Glass with metal tops. $12-15

Pan American World Airways (PanAm, USA). Left set, Taiwan, 1990s, glass with metal tops, $12-15. Other sets from Pan American Airways, 1940s. Center set, cardboard. Right set, plastic. $20-22.

Malaysia Airlines. Japan, 1990s. Noritake, Hibiscus pattern. $25-30.

Malaysia Airlines. Japan, 1990s. Noritake. $25-30.

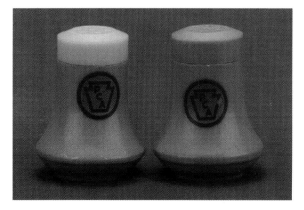

PCA (older Pennsylvania airline with the Keystone in the symbol). 1950s. $18-20.

Malaysian Airline System. Japan, 1980s.
Shown with original box. $12-15.

Northwest Airlines (USA), 1980s. Left set, Japan, $18-20. Right set, glass with metal tops, $8-10.

Northwest. 1960s. Cardboard. $20-22.

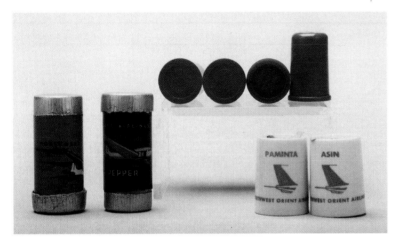

Left:
Northwest. 1950s.
Cardboard. $20-22.

Northwest. 1960s. Top sets, plastic, $10-12. Bottom sets, cardboard, $15-18.

Philippine Airlines. 1980s. $25-30.

Northwest. 1980s. Glass with metal tops. $10-12.

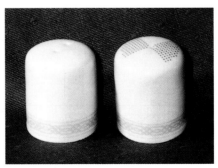

Philippine Airlines. 1980s. Glass with metal tops. $10-12.

Royal Air Moroc (Morocco). 1990s. $20-25.

Republic Airlines (USA). 1970s. Plastic. $10-12.

Qantas Airways (Australia). Left set, Japan, 1980s, Narumi, $25-30. Center shaker, England, 1950s, metal. $15-18. Right shaker, England, 1980s, Wedgwood, $12-15.

Qantas. 1960s. Glass. $15-18.

Qantas. 1950s. Plastic. $15-18.

Sabena Belgian World Airlines. 1990s. Glass with metal tops on plastic tray. $10-12.

Saudia (Saudi Arabia). Japan, 1980s. Noritake. Comes with either green or navy blue band. $30-35.

Royal Brunei Airlines. England, 1980s. Royal Doulton. $30-35.

SAS. USA, 1950s. Cardboard. $22-25.

SAS—Scandinavian Airlines System (Sweden, Denmark and Norway). England, 1980s. Glass shakers with metal tops in plastic holder. $10-12.

SAS. USA, 1960s. Plastic. $18.20.

Singapore Airlines. Japan, 1980s. $22-25.

Thai Airways International (Thailand). 1980s. Metal, turbine engines. $35-40.

South African Airways (Republic of South Africa). China, 1990s. $30-35.

Thai. 1990s. Glass shakers with metal tops in plastic holder. $10-12.

Trans-Canada Air Lines (TCA).
USA, 1970s. Plastic. $10-12.

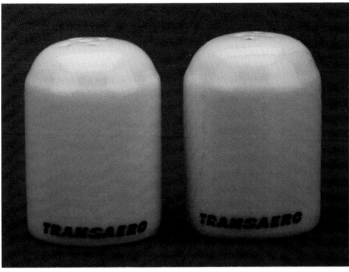

Transaero (USSR).
1960s. $30-35.

Trans World Airlines (TWA, USA).
1950s. Plastic. $15-18.

TWA. 1950s. Plastic and cardboard. $12-15.

TWA. England, 1950s.
Plastic. $12-15.

Turkish Airlines. 1980s.
Plastic. $12-15

Left:
TWA. 1960s. Plastic. $12-15.

19

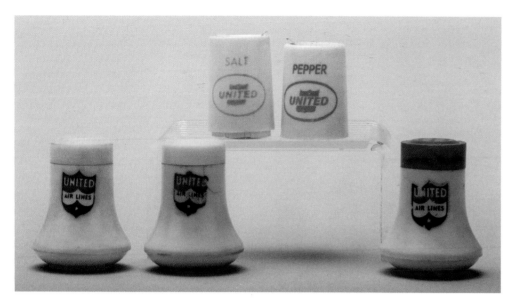

United Airlines (USA). 1960s. Plastic and cardboard. $12-15.

United. 1960s. One-piece plastic set. $22-25.

Emirates Airlines (United Arab Emirates). England, 1980s. $30-35.

United. 1950s. Cardboard. $18-20.

Emirates. England, 1990s. Royal Doulton. $40-45.

Emirates. 3". France, 1990s. Limoges. Shown with original box and card. $65-70.

Union de Transports Aeriens (UTA, France). 1960s. Plastic. $20-22.

US Airways. China, 1990s. Plastic. $8-10.

Varig (Brazil). 1960s. Schmidt. $25-30.

Western Airlines (USA). 1960s. Plastic. $22-25.

Virgin Atlantic Airways (England). Left set, 1980s, Wedgwood, $25-30. Right set, 1990s, plastic, "Pinched from Virgin Atlantic", $25-30.

Left:
Wardair (Canada). USA, 1960s. Plastic. Shown with napkin ring. $18-20.

Right:
Western. 1950s. Cardboard and plastic. $12-15.

AUTOMOBILE-RELATED

PLASTIC GAS PUMPS

All sets were made in the USA and stand about 2.75" high. They were "give-aways" from various gas stations in the 1950s-1960s. Primary location, if known, is indicated.

Left and right: Agway. New York and Pennsylvania. $75-85.

Amlico (American Liberty Oil Company). Texas. $100-110.

Ashland. Illinois, Kentucky, and Ohio. Left set, $150-175. Right set, $100-110.

Right and far right: Amoco. East Coast. $50-55.

Atlantic. $40-45.

Barney's. Illinois. $150-175.

Bay. Midwest and East Coast. $75-85.

Best. $200+.

Calso (California Standard Oil). $100-110.

Carter. Nebraska, Montana, and Idaho. $200+.

Champlin. Midwest. $100-110.

Chevron. $150-175.

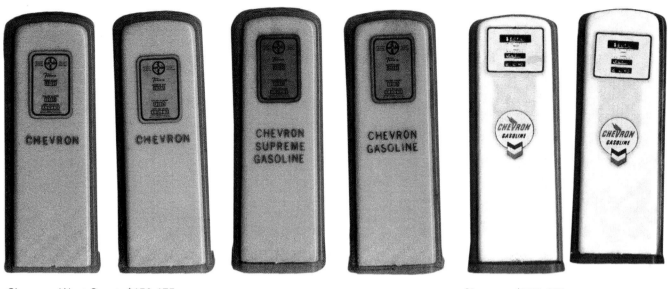

Chevron. West Coast. $150-175.

Chevron. $150-175.

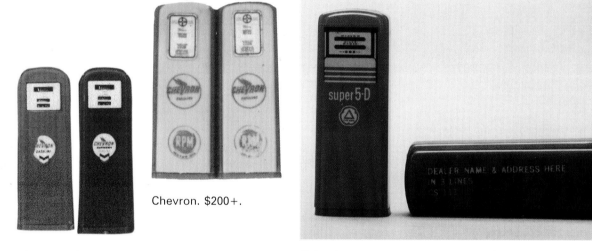

Chevron. $200+.

Chevron. $150-175.

Cities Service. Salesman's sample. $40-45.

Cities Service. Left set, $50-55. Right set, $40-45.

Cities Service. $40-45.

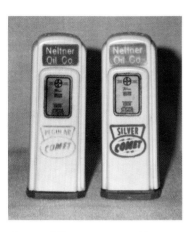

Comet. Minnesota and Wisconsin. $150-175.

Conoco. $30-35.

Co Op. $150-175.

Co Op. $50-55.

Co Op. Farmers Union. $150-175.

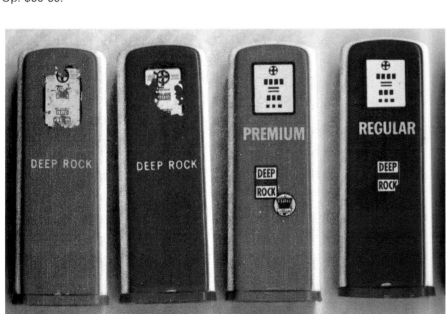

Deep Rock. $150-175.

Deep Rock. Illinois, Missouri, and Wisconsin. $100-110.

Derby. $150-175.

DX Ethyl. $75-85.

Derby. $100-110.

DX Boron. $50-55.

DX Boron. $50-55.

Economy. Rare. $250+.

El Paso. Texas. $150-175.

Farmers Union Co-Op. Midwest. $200+.

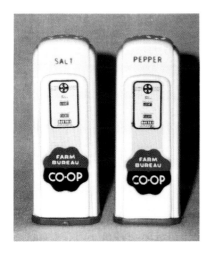

Farm Bureau Co-Op. $100-110.

Esso. Left set, $12-15. Right set, $30-35.

Flying A. $150-175.

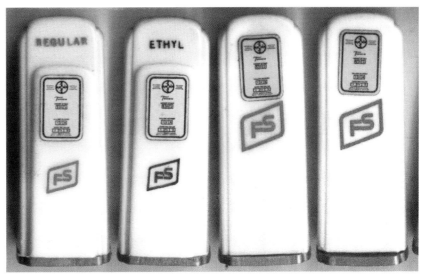

FS. Midwest. $100-110.

Flying A. $50-55.

Fina. Southwest. $50-55.

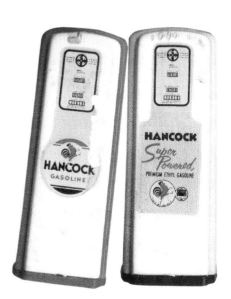

Hancock. California. $150-175.

Gulf. Left set, $75-85. Right set, $50-55.

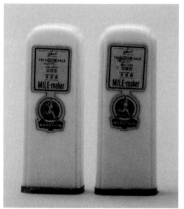

Marathon. $50-55.

Midland. Wisconsin and Michigan. Co-Op. $150-175.

Kendall. $200+.

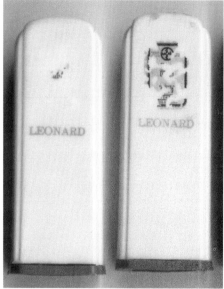

Leonard. $200+.

Mileage. Minnesota, Nebraska, and Wisconsin. $150-175.

Mobil. $30-35.

Mobil. Left set, $100-110. Right set, $150-175.

Pacific. California. $75-85.

Pennzoil. $200+.

Pure. $40-45.

Phillips 66. $30-35.

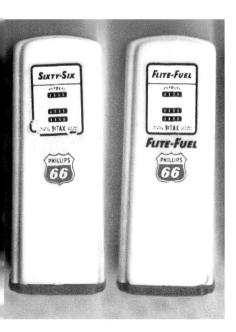

Phillips 66. Left set, $20-25. Right set, $12-15.

Phillips 66. $75-85.

Pan-Am. Texas and Louisiana. $200+.

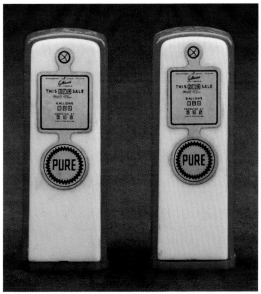

Pure. $40-45.

Richfield. $150-175.

Richfield Ethyl. $150-175.

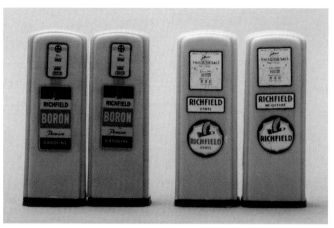

Richfield. Left set, $150-175. Right set, $50-55.

Richfield. $100-110.

Shell. Left set, $40-45. Center set, $50-55. Right set, $30-35.

Sico. $150-175.

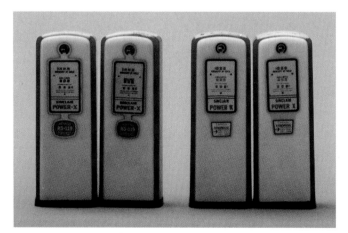

Sinclair. $40-45.

Signal. California. $150-175.

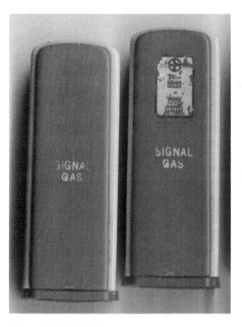

Signal. $150-175.

Skelly. $40-45.

Skelly. $150-175.

Skelly. $150-175.

Snider. Minnesota. $200+.

Sohio. $100-110.

Standard Oil of Kentucky.
$150-175.

Standard. $50-55.

Standard. Left set, $75-85. Right set, $40-45.

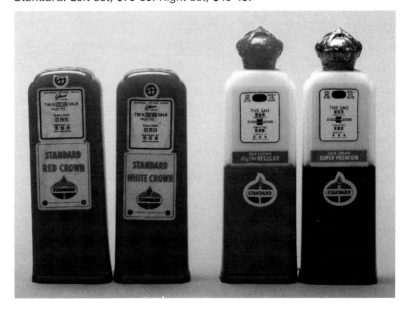

31

Union 76. California. $100-110.

Sunoco. $30-35.

Universal. $100-110.

Texaco. Left set, $150-175. Right set, $20-25.

Zingo. Indiana. $200+.

Zenith. $200+.

Zephyr. $150-175.

Zephyr. $150-175.

OTHER GASOLINE-RELATED

Frontier. 3.25". USA, 1950s.
Messer Pottery. $250-275.

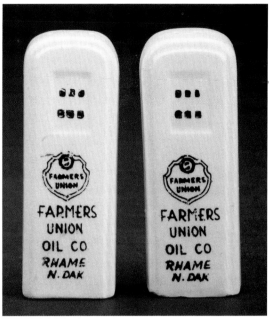

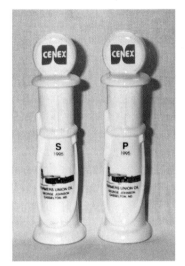

Farmers Union. 3.5". USA, 1950s. Messer
Pottery. $200-225.

Cenex. 6". USA, 1990s. $20-25.

Texaco. 4". China, 1990s. Enesco. $12-15.

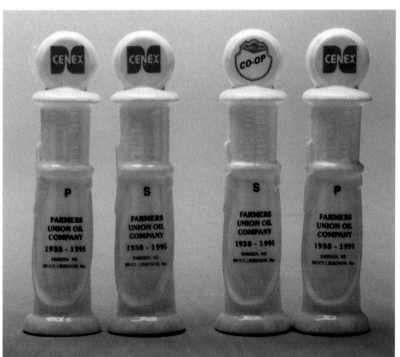

Cenex/Farmers Union Co-Op. 6". USA, 1990s. $20-25.

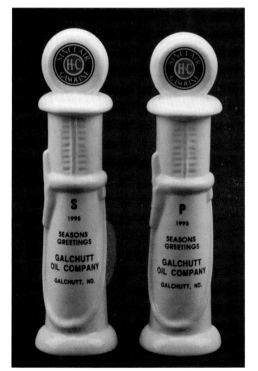

Sinclair. 6". USA, 1990s. $20-25.

Amco. 1.25". USA, 1950s. Plastic. $12-15.

Chevron. 4". USA, 1950s. Shown with original sleeve. $20-25.

Enco Humble Oil and Refining Co. 2.25". USA, 1950s. Wood and metal. $12-15.

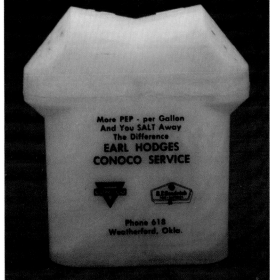

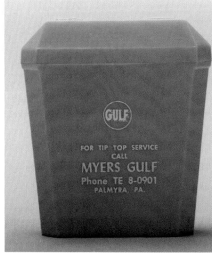

Earl Hodges Conoco Services, Ohio. 4". USA. 1960s. One-piece plastic set. $12-15.

Left:
Gulf. 4". USA, 1950s. One-piece plastic set. $12-15.

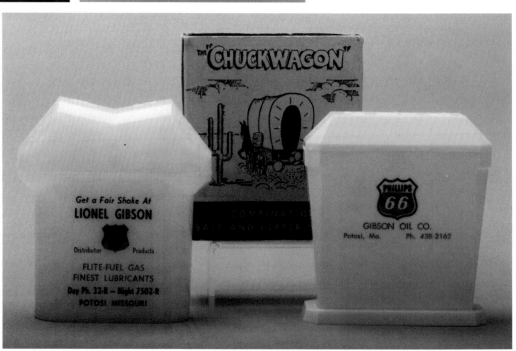

Phillips 66. 4". USA, 1950s. Plastic. Shown with original sleeve. $12-15.

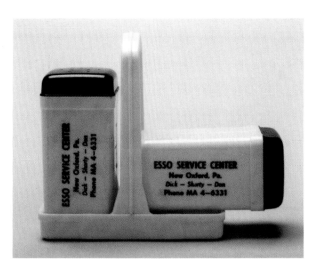

Esso Service Center, New Oxford, Pennsylvania.
3.75". USA, 1950s. Plastic. $8-10.

Esso. 2.75". USA, 1950s. Milk glass with metal tops. $30-35.

Esso. 3.25". USA, 1950s. Plastic. $12-15.

Esso. 2.5". USA, 1960s. One-piece plastic set. $8-10.

Esso. 4". USA, 1950s. One-piece plastic set. $12-15.

Esso. 3.5". Canada, 1980s. Glass with plastic tops. $8-10.

Mobilgas. 2.5". USA, 1950s.
Milford Pottery by Klay Kraft.
One-piece ceramic set. $75-
85.

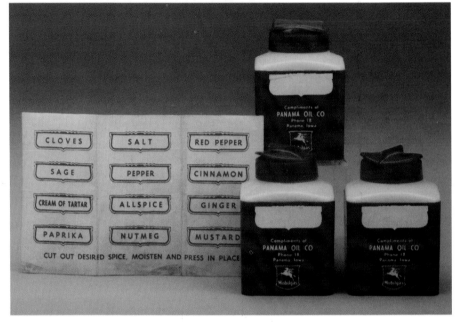

Mobilgas. 3". USA, 1950s. Plastic.
Panama Oil Co., Panama, Iowa. Promotion with various labels to be placed on
the shakers. $12-15.

Mobil "Friendly Farm" summer and
winter scenes. 3.25". USA, 1950s.
Carter Hoffman, California. Shown
with original box. Matches
dinnerware given away by Mobil
dealers. $25-30.

Sinclair. 3". USA, 1950s. Plastic. $8-10.

Shell. 3.25". USA, 1950s. One-piece plastic set. $12-15.

Shell. 4". Canada, 1950s. One-piece plastic set. $12-15.

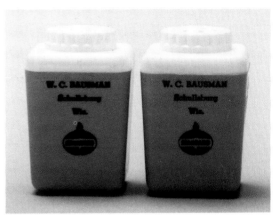

Standard. 2.25". USA, 1950s. Plastic. $8-10.

Standard. 2.5". USA, 1950s. Plastic. $8-10.

Dikkers & Burkholder Texaco Service, Freeport, Illinois. 4.5". USA, 1950s. Glass with plastic tops. $22-25.

Standard. 3.75". USA, 1950s. Glass with metal tops. $25-30.

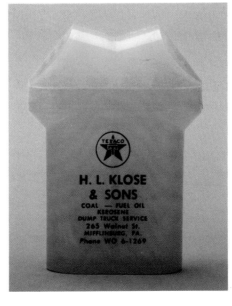

Texaco. 3.25". USA, 1950s. One-piece plastic set. $12-15.

Left:
Esso Multi-Purpose grease. 4". USA, 1950s. Cardboard and plastic. $10-12.

Right:
Purolator Oil Filters. 1.5". USA, 1950s. Cardboard. $8-10.

Far right:
Quaker State Motor Oil. 1.5". USA, 1950s. Cardboard. $8-10.

Left:
Uniflo Motor Oil. 1.5". USA. Cardboard. $8-10.

Right:
Beachley's Car Radio Center, Harrisburg, Pennsylvania. 2". USA, 1950s. Plastic. $6-8.

Newport Auto Parts Inc., Newport, Pennsylvania. 3". USA, 1950s. Plastic. $6-8.

Seibring Tires, Taylor Tire Co. 4". USA, 1950s. Glass with plastic tops. $25-30.

GM Fisher Body. 3.5". USA, 1980s. Glass, 75th Anniversary. $10-12.

Bolta General Tires. 4". USA, 1950s. Plastic. $12-15.

Left:
Michelin Tires. 4". Japan, 1990s. Made for the Japanese market. $50-60.

Firestone/US Rubber Tires. 2.25". Japan, 1960s. $22-25.

Korn Buick/Jeep, Kalispell, Montana.
4". USA, 1950s. One-piece plastic set.
$10-12.

Dauby Motor Co Inc. (reverse side is
Ideal Farm Equipment, Tell City, Indiana).
4". USA, 1950s. One-piece plastic set.
$10-12.

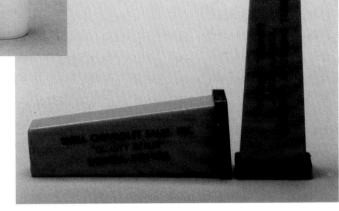

Right:
Chevrolet. 3".
USA, 1950s.
Plastic. $8-10.

Chevrolet. 1.75". USA, 1950s. Plastic. $6-8.

Chevrolet. 2.75". USA, 1950s. Plastic. $50-55.

Left:
Ben Hur Ford. 3.5". USA, 1960s.
Plastic. $6-8.

Left:
Chevrolet
Corvette. 2".
China, 1990s.
Enesco. $12-15.

Right:
Ford. 4". USA,
1950s. One-
piece plastic set.
$12-15.

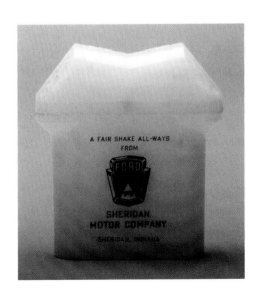

Above and right: VW Delivery Wagon. 4". Japan, 1970s. Also comes in pink. $65-70. With box, $75-80.

Pontiac. Anderson Motor Co., Lyons, Kansas. 3.25". USA, 1960s. One-piece plastic set. $12-15.

Volkswagen Stackers. 2.25". China. Left set, 1968 model. Right set, 1990s model. Enesco prototypes, not produced. Unpriced.

ADAC. 1". Germany, 1990s. All Gemeine Deutsche Automobile Club. Street wrecker or tow truck model. Given away as promotion for joining the club. $35-40.

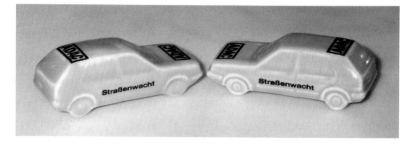

OTHER

Greyhound. 1.5". Japan, 1970s. $25-30.

Greyhound. 3.25". Japan, 1980s. $12-15.

Greyhound 1940s-style Bus. 1". Japan, 1950s. Metal body with rubber tires. $45-50.

Greyhound, Scenic Cruiser models. 1". Japan, 1950s. Metal body with rubber tires. $40-45.

Right:
Amtrak. 3". USA, 1990s. $10-12.

Lionel Train. 1.75". China, 1990s. Enesco. $12-15.

Pennsylvania Railroad. 2.75". USA, 1980s. $8-10.

Left set, B&O Railroad. Right set, Pennsylvania Railroad. 3.75". Canada, 1990s. $8-10.

Rio Grande Scenic Line. 3". USA, 1960s. Private Ceramicist. $12-15.

Air Stream Trailers. 4" USA, 1950s. One-piece plastic set. $12-15.

Serro Scotty Sportsman Camper. 3.75". USA, 1960s. Glass with plastic tops. $6-8.

Left:
Jayco, Inc. Travel Trailers. 4.75". Probably USA, 1970s. Presented as gifts to dealers and employees at the company's annual family reunion in 1972. Approximately 150 sets made. $90-100.

Right:
Lewis Trailer Sales, Pasco, Washington. 4.5". USA, 1950s. Glass with plastic tops. $20-22.

Holland America
Line. 2.25". USA.
Metal with plastic
base. $15-18.

Commodore
Cruise Line. 3".
Norway, 1990s.
$12-15.

Cunard (Cruise Line). 2.75". England, 1980s. Royal
Doulton. $20-25.

White Star Line.
3.5". England,
1950s. $20-25.

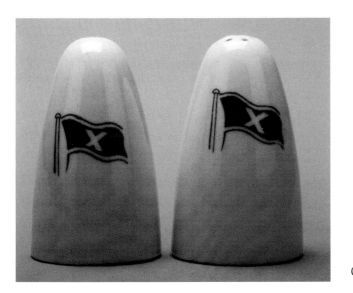

Unknown ship shaker. 2.5". 1950s. Can someone identify
this? Unpriced.

Chandris Lines. 3". England, 1950s. $20-25.

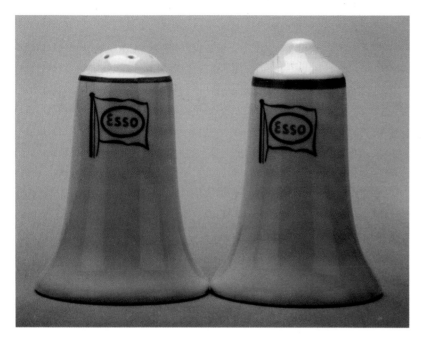

Standard Oil Co. (Esso), multinational. 3.5". England, 1950s. $25-30.

Mack truck. Closeup of the back of the dog.

Mack Truck. 4". USA. 1950s. Marston Co., California. $150-175.

Above and right: Mack Truck Bulldog. 8". USA, 1960s. Salt shaker and pepper mill. "Made on the third planet from the sun." We Bounds Associates, Manhattan Beach, California. $45-50.

70-37 Truck Stop. 3.5". USA, 1960s. Plastic. $ 6-8.

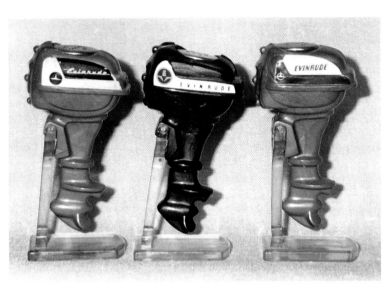 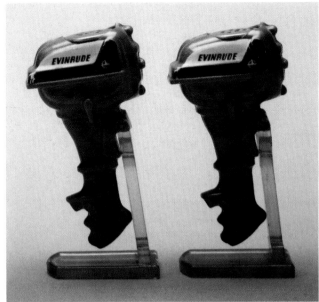

Evinrude Motors. 3.5". USA, 1950s. Metal and plastic. Left photo shows three models produced. Believed to be Christmas gift to company employees. $200-225.

Harley Davidson "Hog" Gas Tanks. 2". China, 1990s. $25-30.

Harley Davidson Oil Cans. 3". China, 1990s. Vandor. $20-22.

Harley Davidson Engine. 4". China, 1990s. Vandor. $20-22.

FARM-RELATED

JOHN DEERE

1998 Heartland Chapter Condiment. 3.75". USA. New Rose Collection. One of a kind #2 set with silver trim. Sold at Club convention for $300. Regular set, $75-80.

Tractor and Wagon. 2.5". China, 1990s. Enesco. $12-15.

1999 Heartland Chapter Condiment. 3". USA, 1990s. New Rose Collection. One of a kind #2 set with silver trim. Sold at Novelty S&P Shakers Club convention for $425. Regular set, $65-70.

1997 Heartland Chapter Nodder. 3.75". USA. New Rose Collection. One of a kind #2 set with silver trim. Sold at Club convention for $600. Regular set, $90-100.

Right:
Glass shakers.
4.5". USA,
1990s. $12-15.

Mid States Fence. Mid States Steel & Wire Co. Crawfordsville, Indiana. 2". USA, 1950s. Plastic. $25-30.

Red Brand Fencing. 3.25". USA, 1960s. $45-50.

Harvestore Silos. 4.5". USA, 1960s. Three models shown. $25-30.

New Idea Equipment. Dauby Motor Co. Inc. 4". USA, 1950s. One-piece plastic set. $12-15.

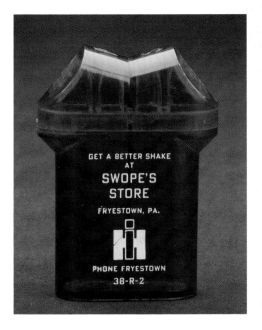

Left: International Harvester. Swope's Store. 3". USA, 1950s. One-piece plastic set. $12-15.

Right: Madison Elevators. 4.75". USA, 1960s. $40-45.

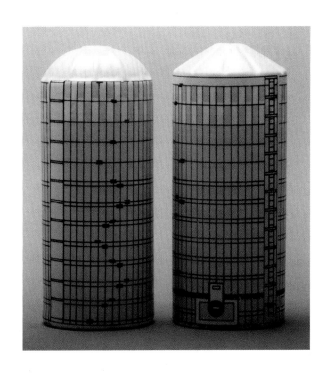

47

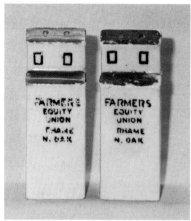

Grain Elevators. 3.25". USA, 1950s. Messer Pottery.
Farmer's Equity Union, $100-125. Others, $125-150.

Clark County Farmers Elevator. 2.75". USA, 1990s. $6-8.

The Quaker Oats Co. Grain Elevators. 3". Japan, 1960s. $6-8.

Keltgen Grain Elevators. 2.75". USA, 1990s. $6-8.

Kent Seed. Brown's Grain and Feed. 4.25". USA, 1950s. $10-12.

FS (Farm Supply). Woodford County Seed Co. 3.75". USA, 1960s. One-piece plastic set. $12-15.

Butte Feeds. 3". Brazil, 1990s.
$10-12.

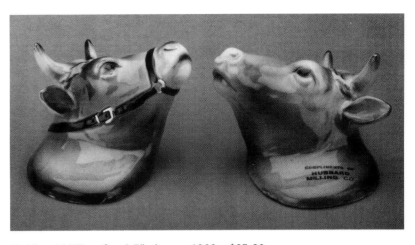

Hubbard Milling Co. 2.5". Japan, 1960s. $25-30.

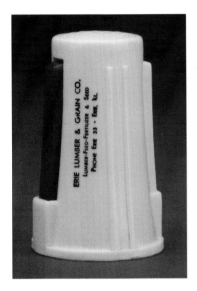

Erie Lumber & Grain Co., Erie, Illinois. 4". USA,
1950s. One-piece plastic set. $10-12.

Lennox Co-Op Ass'n. Lennox, South Dakota. 4.5". USA, 1950s.
Puritan Pottery. $35-40.

Indian Maid Feeds. 4.25". Japan, 1960s. Meriden
& Owatonna on ends of base. $75-80.

Farmwell Feeds. 3.75". Japan, 1970s. $50-55.

DeKalb Feeds Profit Pullets. "DeKalb is a Good Egg". 2.5". USA, 1950s. Plastic. $6-8.

Purina, Courtesy Your Purina Dealer. 2.5". USA, 1950s. Plastic. $6-8.

Bill Rice Ranch, Murfreesboro, Tennesee. 2.75". China, 1990s. $6-8.

Potatoes. "N. Dak. State Seed Dept". 2". USA, 1950s. Rosemeade Pottery. $225-250.

Red River Valley All-Purpose Potatoes. 2.5". USA, 1950s. Plastic. $30-35.

Potatoes. "Compliments of L.E. Tibert Co". 1.75". USA, 1950s. Rosemeade Pottery. $225-250.

Farmers Hybrid Corn Seed.
4.75". USA, 1950s. $8-10.

Trojan, Northern Bred Corn Seed. 3".
Japan, 1950s. $35-40.

Trojan Corn Seed. 4.75". USA, 1950s.
Rosemeade Pottery. $250-275.

Pfister Hybrids-Associated
Pfister Growers. 1.75". USA,
1950s. Pushbutton, plastic.
$8-10.

Trojan. 2.25". Japan, 1960s. $10-12.

Pfister Hybrids. 2.25". USA, 1950s. Plastic. $6-8.

Marlo Seed Co. 2.75". China, 1990s. $8-10.

FOOD

Left:
Aunt Jemima and
Uncle Mose. 3.5".
USA, 1940s. F&F
Mold & Die Works,
Dayton, Ohio. $25-30.

Right:
Aunt Jemima and
Uncle Mose. 5.25".
USA, 1940s. F&F
Mold & Die Works.
$40-45.

Left:
Betty Crocker flour
sacks. 2.5". USA,
1950s. Chalkware.
$20-22.

Right:
Blue Bonnet Sue. 5".
Taiwan, 1980s.
Benjamin & Medwin,
New York. $30-35.

BORDEN'S

Elsie stacker. 4". USA, 1960s.
$45-50.

Elsie stacker. 3.75". USA,
1960s. $40-45.

Elmer. 3.5". USA, 1960s. $35-40.

Elsie & Elmer. 4". USA, 1980s. Copyright Borden's. Composition material. $65-70.

Elsie & Elmer. 4". USA, 1960s. $50-55.

Elsie's Twins. 3.5". Japan, 1960s. 3 sets. $18-20.

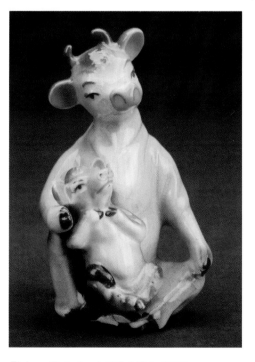

Elsie with twin. 4.75". USA, 1950s. Ceramic Arts Studio. $85-90.

Elsie with her twins, Beulah and Beauregard. 4-5". Japan, 1960s. $40-45.

Sourdough Jake and his mule. 4". Japan, 1960s. $65-70.

Stroehmann Bread. 3.5". USA, 1950s. Plastic. $8-10.

Sourdough Jake. 3.75". Japan, 1960s. ©Kelvin. $65-70.

Dick Bros. Bread. 3.5". USA, 1950s. Lenox. $25-30.

Holsum Bread. 3". USA, 1950s. Plastic. $8-10.

McVitie's Biscuits. 5.5". England, 1970s. $20-25.

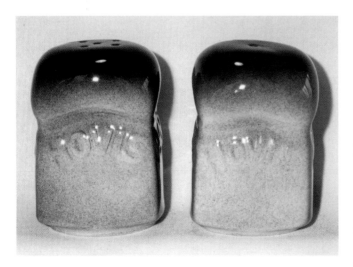

Hovis Bread. 2.75". England, 1950s. Carltonware. $45-50.

Festa Italiana. 4".
USA, 1970s. $8-10.

Crawford's Cheese Specials. 3.25". USA,
1960s. $20-25.

Star Valley Swiss
Cheese. 2.5". USA,
1950s. Ceramic Arts
Studio. Only licensed
advertising set made by
CAS. $40-45.

Euclid Coffee Co.
Cleveland, OH.
6.25". USA. 1950s.
Glass with metal
tops. $20-25.

Luzianne Coffee or Tea Mammy Twins. 5.25". USA, 1950s.
F&F Mold & Die Works. Premium for 3 vouchers and fifty
cents per set. $125-135.

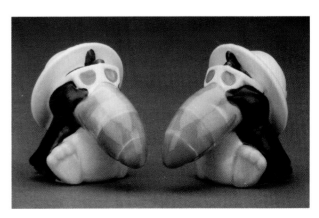

Left:
Java Coffee Mills, Chi-
cago. 3.5". USA, 1940s.
Antique glass. $15-18.

Right:
Fruit Loops, Toucan Sam.
3". Korea, 1980s. Josef
Originals. $40-45.

CAMPBELL'S SOUP

4.25" USA. Plastic. F&F Mold & Die Works. Permission of Campbell Soup Company. $30-35.

3.5". USA. ©1982. Campbell Kids Collection. $25-30.

5". China. ©CSC 1998. Benjamin & Medwin. $12-15.

Tins. 3.75". China. 1990s. $8-10.

Barbecue. 4". Possibly USA, 1990s. $18-20.

2.75". China, 1990s. $8-10.

4.25". China, © 1998.
™©Campbell Soup Company.
Available only through mail-in
offer. $25-30.

Pepper Pot salt shaker and pepper mill.
5.75". USA, 1960s. Wood. $20-25.

3". China, 1990s. ©CSC. $15-18.

5". China, 1990s. $12-15.

4". China, ©1996 Campbell Soup Company.
$15-18.

Left:
Cracker Jack,
Sailor Jack and
Bingo. 2.75".
Japan, 1960s.
$20-25.

Right:
Cracker Jack. 4".
China, 1997.
©Bordens. $35-
40.

Cream of Wheat. 4.5". Japan, 1960s. $50-55.

Cream of Wheat. 2". USA, 1960s. $35-40.

Heinz Ketchup. 4". Hong Kong, 1970s. Plastic. $6-8.

Famous Amos Cookies. Chip & Cookie. 4". Indonesia, 1990s. Fitz & Floyd. $25-28.

Heinz Ketchup. 3.25". Probably Japan, 1970s. $150+.

Heinz. 3.5". USA, 1990s. Glass with metal tops. $10-12.

HOME PRIDE BREAD: FLOUR FRED

Above left:
Condiment. 4.25". England, 1979. $65-75.

Above right:
3". England, 1980s. Plastic. $20-25.

Right:
4.25" & 3.25". England, 1980s. Plastic. $20-25.

Below:
4.5". England, 1990s. $60-65.

4.25". England, 1980s. Plastic. $30-35.

HERSHEY CHOCOLATE

Cocoa Bean Babies. 2". Germany, 1930s. $250.+.

Cows. 2.5". Japan, 1980s. Shown with original box. $50-55.

Pigs in Trough. 3.25". Japan, 1980s. $50-55.

Kisses. 2.5-3". USA. 1960s. Left set, © Happiness Inc., Kingman, Kansas. Right set, Black Hills China and Ceramics, Sturgis, South Dakota. $12-15.

Baking Chocolate. 4". Japan, 1970s. $15-18.

Milk Chocolate mugs. 3.5". Japan, 1970s. $12-15.

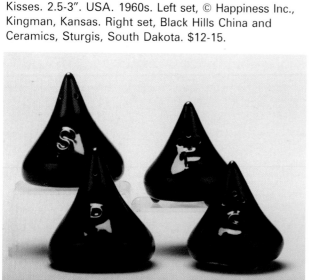

Cylinders. 2.75". Japan, 1980s. $20-25.

Dutch Couple in Boat. 4". Japan, 1980s. $125-150.

Houses. 3.75". Japan, ©1982 Hershey Foods Inc. Shown with original box. $70-75.

Cylinders. 2.75". Japan, 1960s. $12-15.

Tins. 4". Taiwan, 1980s. $8-10.

Chocolate, Golden Harvest. 3.25". USA. Glass with metal tops. $6-8.

ICE CREAM

Foster's Freeze. 4". Japan, 1960s. $12-15.

Dairy Queen Girls. 3.75". Japan, 1964. ™Dairy Queen. $75-80.

Dairy Queen. 5". China, 1998. $12-15.

Dairy Queen. 4.25". Japan, 1970s. $12-15.

Right:
Sweety. 3".
Probably Japan,
1970s. $22-25.

Safe-T. 3". Japan, 1970s. $12-15.

Tee & Eff with basket. 3.5". Japan, 1970s. Note factory error in name on right set (no "Tee"). $20-25.

Far left:
Safe-T Pacific. 3.5". USA, 1970s. $12-15.

Left:
Tee & Eff. 3.5". Japan, 1970s. Enesco. Note "Tastee Freeze" under the names. $30-35.

Right:
Tastee. 3.5". Japan, 1970s. $12-15.

Far right:
Midget. 3". Japan, 1970s. $12-15.

Left and far left:
Yum-ee-Yum Ice Cream. 2.75". Japan. ©Imports Inc. Front and back views. $55-60.

Jolly Green Giant. 4". Taiwan, 1990s. Benjamin & Medwin. $20-25.

Jolly Green Giant. 4". Japan, 1980s. $55-60.

Keebler Elves. 4.5". Taiwan, 1980s. Benjamin & Medwin. $25-30.

Kellogg's Snap & Pop. 2.5". Japan, 1960s. $25-30.

Florida Oranges. 1.5". Probably Japan, 1970s. Copyright Sun-Glo Products Co Inc. $12-15.

Rawling's Mixing Water & Fruit Juices. 4". England, 1980s. $20-25.

Mary Kitchen Corn Beef
Hash, Hormel Foods. 3".
Taiwan, 1990s. Mail-in offer.
$15-18.

Montana Beef. 3.5". Italy, 1960s. $12-15.

Perdue chicken. 2.5". USA, 1970s.
$8-10.

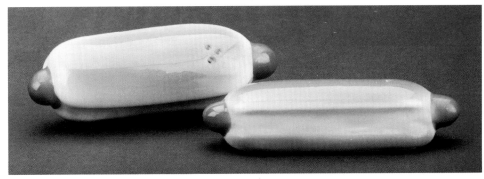

Pez. 4".China, 1990s. $20-22.

Busch Famous Sausage. 1". USA, 1940s. Top and bottom views. $18-20.

Girl on yellow chair. 4". China. ©Mars, 1997. $ 25-30

"Nuts" & "I'm Baad". 3.5". China, 1990s. Benjamin & Medwin. $15-18.

2.5" England, 1970s. Carltonware. $65-75.

"Cool Blue" & "I Melt for No One". 3.5". China, 1990s. Benjamin & Medwin. $15-18.

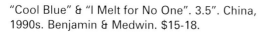

Girl on blue chair. 4.25". Thailand, 1990s. Copyright Mars. $25-30.

MR. PEANUT

Left and below:
4". USA, 1950s. Plastic. Note: Red and cream color set appears to be original paint. $18-20.

Left:
4.5". Japan, 1960s. Ceramic with rhinestone monocle. $70-75.

Right:
3". Japan, 1960s. Ceramic. $80-85.

Black and tan. 4". USA, 1950s. Plastic. $15-18.

4.25". Japan, 1990s. Ceramic. $10-12.

3.25". USA, 1950s. Plastic. $10-12.

5.5". Taiwan. 1990s. Glass. $8-10.

Right:
3.25". USA. 1950s. Left set shown in original package. Plastic. $10-12.

Below:
5". Taiwan. ©PLC 1990. Benjamin & Medwin. Ceramic. $15-18.

5.5". China, 1990s. Glass. $8-10.

4". USA, 1950s. Plastic. $25-30.

PILLSBURY

Left:
Poppin' Fresh &
Poppie. 4". USA.
1974. Plastic. $20-22.

Right:
Poppin' Fresh &
Poppie. 4.25". Japan,
1990s. Made for
Japanese market.
$30-35.

All-American Pillsbury Dough Boy. 3". China,
1990s. Benjamin & Medwin. $12-15.

Poppin' Fresh. 3.5". Japan, 1960s. $15-18.

Poppin' Fresh. 3.5". Probably Japan,
1960s. $12-15.

Pillsbury's Best. 4.5". Taiwan, 1970s. $10-12.

Pillsbury's Best. 4.25". Taiwan, 1990s. Benjamin & Medwin. $12-15.

Pillsbury Dough Boys. 4". China, 1990s. Benjamin & Medwin. $12-15.

Pillsbury Dough Boy & Flour sack. 4". China, 1990s. Benjamin & Medwin. $12-15.

Pillsbury Dough Boy with cookies. 4". China, 1990s. Benjamin & Medwin. $12-15.

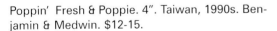

Poppin' Fresh & Poppie. 4". Taiwan, 1990s. Benjamin & Medwin. $12-15.

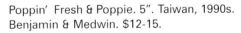

Poppin' Fresh & Poppie. 5". Taiwan, 1990s. Benjamin & Medwin. $12-15.

71

Red River Red. All-purpose Potatoes. Red. White. Russets. 4.25". Japan. Red River Valley. $90-100.

Idaho Spudette. 4.75". USA, 1960s. Private Ceramicist. $25-30.

Red River Red as a red potato. Pair, $120-125.

Right:
Ragu. 3.25". China, 1990s. Mail-in Offer. $12-15.

Smith's Potato Chips. 3". England, 1960s. $20-25.

Rice A Roni. 1.75". China, 1990s. Mail-in Offer. $10-12.

Right:
The New Era Potato Chips. 3.25". USA, 1970s. ©Decoware. Metal Cans. $20-25.

Quaker Oats. 4". USA, 1960s.
Plastic. $120-125.

Premium Saltine Crackers. 3".
Taiwan, 1990s. Mail-in offer. $6-8.

Quaker Oats. 3.75". England, 1970s. Wood's. Promotion with
coupon. $120-125.

Nabisco Premium Plus Crackers. 3.5". USA, 1950s. Plastic. $12-15.

Nabisco Premium Crackers. 2". USA, 1950s.
Chalkware. $12-15.

Nissin Noodles. 2.75". Japan, 1990s. Made for the Japanese market. $30-35.

Diamond Crystal Salt. .5". Probably USA, 1950s. Metal. $10-12.

Sterling Salt. 1.5". USA, 1950s. Cardboard. $8-10.

Sno-White Salt & Crown Colony Pepper. 1.5". USA, 1950s. Plastic. $8-10.

Leslie Salt. 1.5". USA. 1950s. Cardboard. Leslie Salt Co., San Francisco. $8-10.

Windsor Salt Co. Ltd. 1.5". Canada, 1950s. Cardboard. $8-10.

Carey Salt. 1.5". USA, 1950s. Cardboard. $6-8 each.

Carey Iodized Salt. 1.5". USA, 1950s. Carey Salt Company, Hutchinson, Kansas. Cardboard. Single, $3-4, 6-pack $18-20.

Morton Salt. 3.75". USA, 1980s. Cardboard. $6-8

Morton Salt. 1.5". USA, 1980s. Cardboard. $6-8.

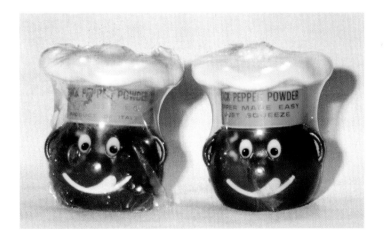

Black Pepper Powder. 2.25". Italy, 1960s. Plastic. Packed in Italy for Dalt Int'l Inc. Englewood Cliffs, New Jersey. "Pepper made easy. Just squeeze". $10-12.

SAUCES

Tabasco. 3". Taiwan, 1980s. McIlhenny Co. $10-12.

Tabasco Pepper Sauce. 2.75". Taiwan, 1990s. ©Tabasco. McIlhenny Co. $12-15.

La Choy Soy Sauce. 3". USA, 1950s. Div of Beatrice Foods Co., Archibald, OH. $10-12.

Henri's Dressing. 2.5". USA, 1950s. Glass with metal tops. $8-10.

Watkin's Vanilla & Black Pepper, Winnona, Minnesota. 3.5". USA, 1990s. $10-12.

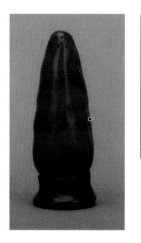

Left and above: Powdered Tabasco. McIlhenny. 3.75". USA, 1960s. $18-20.

Sunshine Baking Company. 2.5". Japan, 1960s. $12-15.

Bisto Gravy Kids, RHM Foods, Ltd. 4.5". England, 1980s. Wade. $175+

Tetley Tea. 3.5". England, 1990s. $25-30.

Left:
Tetley Tea Men. Sidney & Gaffer. 4". England, 1996. Wade. $45-50.

Right:
Tetley Tea Men. 4". England, 1990s. Wade. $45-50.

RESTAURANTS

BOB'S BIG BOY

Big Boy & Dolly. 5". USA, 1990s. Wolfe Studio. Trademark of Elias Brothers Restaurants. $50-55.

Big Boy emerging from an egg. 4". USA, 1990s. Wolfe Studio. Trademark Elias Brothers Restaurants. $50-55.

Original Big Boys. 4.25". Japan, 1960s. 6, 5 and 7 rows of checks. $120-125.

Big Boy and burger. 5.25". USA, 1990s. Wolfe Studio. TM. $40-45.

Big Boy and burger. 4.5". China. Special 1995 Ltd edition. ©EBR Inc. $20-25.

Valentine Big Boy & Dolly. 5". USA, 1990s. Wolfe Studio. $250+.

Fourth of July Big Boy & Dolly. 5.75". USA, 1990s. Wolfe Studio. $90-95.

Halloween Big Boy & Dolly. 4.75". USA, 1990s. Wolfe Studio. Trademark of Elias Brothers Restaurants. $50-55.

Christmas Big Boy & Dolly. 5.75". USA, 1990s. Wolfe Studio. Trademark of Elias Brothers Restaurants. $50-55.

Left:
Big Boy Seasoning Salt. 3.75". USA, 1960s. Plastic. $8-10.

Right:
Big Boy Mugs. 4". USA, 1990s. $20-25.

Big Boys. 4.25". China. ©EBR Inc. Special 1996 Limited Edition—60 years with Big Boy. $18-20.

Millennium Big Boy & Dolly. 5.25". USA, 1990s. Wolfe Studio. $50-55.

Left:
Big Boy Mugs. 4". USA, 1990s. $20-25.

The A.Q. Chicken House, Springdale, Arkansas. 2.25". USA, 1950s. $6-8.

Bob Evans Restaurant. 3". USA, 1990s. $6-8.

Arby's Seasoned Salt. 4.25". USA, 1950s. Glass with metal lid. $8-10.

Dinah's Shack, Palo Alto, California. 2.75". Japan, 1950s. $90-100.

Bonanza Steak House. 2". USA, 1960s. Plastic. $6-8.

Burger Chef. 3.5". USA, 1960s. Plastic. $6-8.

Bonanza Sirloin Pit. 3". Canada, 1960s. Glass with plastic tops. $8-10.

Bon Appetit. 4". Korea, 1980s. Josef Originals. $20-25.

Colony House, Iowa. 3.75". USA, 1950s. $8-10.

Capt. Starns Restaurant, Atlantic City, New Jersey. 3.25". USA, 1950s. Plastic. $12-15.

Checkerboard Café, Mission, South Dakota. 4.25". USA, 1950s. Messer Pottery. $350-375.

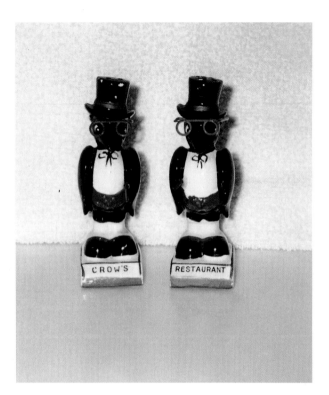

Crow's Restaurant, Galveston, Texas. 4.5". USA, 1950s. $250+.

Above right and right:
The Brown Derby, Hollywood, CA. 1.75". USA, 1950s. $30-35. With original box, $45-50.

Left:
Cracker Barrel. 2.75". China. ©1996 FSD Inc. Old Country Store. $6-8.

Right:
Cracker Barrel. 4". USA, 1980s. PCA. Old Country Store. $6-8.

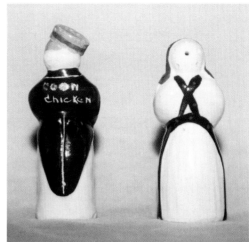

Coon Chicken Inn. 4". Probably USA, 1940s. Front and back views.
A chain of restaurants in the Northwest known for their Southern
fried chicken. $150-160.

Henny Penny Restaurants. 2". USA, 1950s. Chain
of restaurants specializing in broasted chicken.
$18-20.

Right:
Cliff House, San
Francisco. 3.25".
USA, 1960s. $15-18.

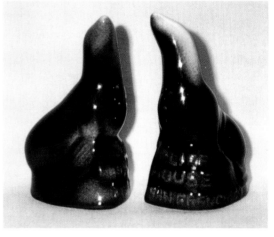

Eddie Bohn. 3.75". USA, 1940s. A BBQ restaurant in Colorado. $20-22.

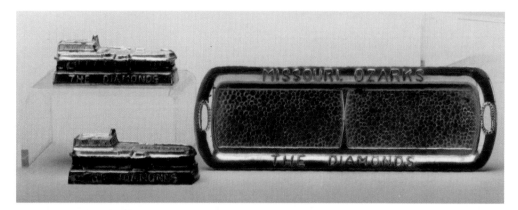

The Diamonds Restaurant. 1". Japan, 1950s. The Diamonds was known as "The World's Largest Roadside Restaurant." It still stands at the intersection of Route 66 and US 50 near Villa Ridge, Missouri. Now known as the Tri-County Truck Stop. $55-60.

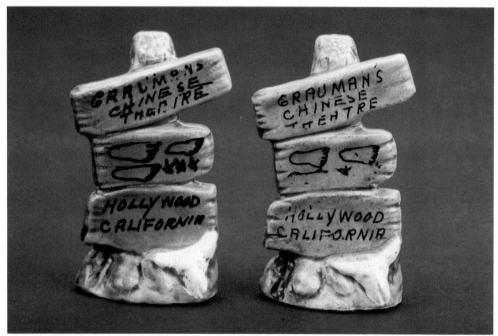

Lambert's Café. 3.25". China, 1990s. Only Home of Throwed Rolls. $6-8.

Grauman's Chinese Theater, Hollywood, California. 3.5". USA, 1950s. $8-10.

Fisherman's Grotto, San Francisco. 3-4.5". Japan, 1970s. Center set is metal, $15-18. Other sets, $12-15.

Machine Shed Restaurant. 6". USA, 1990s. A Midwestern chain. $20-22.

Flying Saucer Restaurants. 2". USA, 1950s. $15-18.

Ideal Fish Restaurant, Santa Cruz, California. 4". USA, 1950s. $20-22.

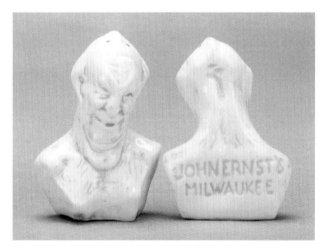

John Ernst's Tavern, Milwaukee, Wisconsin. 3.5". USA, 1950s. Private Ceramicist. $25-30.

The Hot & Kold Shops. 4.25-4.5". USA, 1950s. Left set, composition material. Right set, plastic. $40-45.

Howard Johnson. 3.75". USA, 1990s. Wolfe Studio. 75th Anniversary. Copyright Cendent. $50-55.

The Lighthouse, Norwalk, Connecticut. 3". China, 1990s. $8-10.

KFC: KENTUCKY FRIED CHICKEN

Tops Drive In. 3". USA, 1960s. Glass with plastic tops. $25-30.

Colonel Sanders. 4.25". Canada, 1980s. Plastic. Note: right set with red base is hard to find, $30-35. Other set, $18-20.

3.5". USA, 1970s. Left set, glass with plastic tops. Right set, plastic. $12-15.

Colonel Sanders. 4.75". USA, 1960s. $120-125.

Mini Mills. 3.5". USA, 1970s. Int. Spice Inc. $12-15.

Tops Drive In, Home of the Sir Loiner and Kentucky Fried Chicken. 3.5". USA, 1950s. $25-30.

Colonel and Mrs. Sanders. 4". USA. © Margardt Corp 1972. $25-30.

Colonel Sanders. 3.25". Japan, 1990s. Made for Japanese market. $35-40.

2.5". Japan, 1950s. $20-25.

Left and above:
Little Joe's Restaurant and Grocery, Los Angeles, California. 3.75". USA, 1960s. $12-15.

MCDONALD'S

3.5". China. ©1999 McDonald's Corporation. Treasure Craft. $18-20.

Big Mac and Fries. 3.5". China. ©1997 McDonald's Corporation. Treasure Craft. $18-20.

Right:
3.5". USA, 1990s. Redwing Pottery. $30-35.

Speedy Fries and Milk Shake. 4.5". China. ©1999 McDonald's Corporation. Treasure Craft. $18-20.

3.5". USA, 1990s. Redwing Pottery. $30-35.

Mauna Loa. 3.5". Japan, 1950s. Designed by Mauna Loa, Detroit. $12-15.

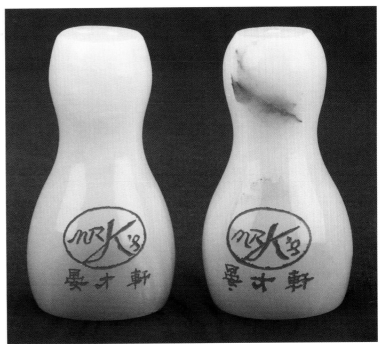

Mr. K's. 3.5". Japan, 1960s. Marble. $8-10.

Pecan Joe's, Newburg, Missouri. 2.5". USA. 1960s. $8-10.

The Pink House, Genoa, Nevada. 4". USA, 1960s. "A meal without fresh spices is like a bride without charm." $8-10.

Pickin' Chicken. 2.5". USA, 1960s. $20-25.

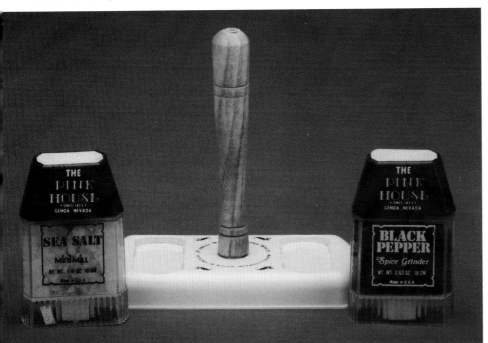

Parker's Cafe. Wedowee, Alabama. 4". USA, 1950s. Plastic. $6-8.

Planet Hollywood. 3.5". China, 1990s. $20-25.

Pioneer Take Out Chicken. 3.5". USA, 1990s. Plastic. $6-8.

Planet Hollywood. 3.75". Canada, 1990s. Glass with metal tops. $8-10.

Red Bull Inn. 3". USA, 1970s. Milk glass with metal tops. $6-8.

Ponderosa Steak House. 3.5". USA, 1960s. Plastic. $6-8.

Roseanne and Tom's Big Food Diner, Eldon, Iowa. 3.5". USA, 1990s. $10-12.

Red Horse Inn. 4". Probably Japan, 1950s. $6-8.

RAINFOREST CAFÉ

Rio Parrot and Iggy Iguana. 4.25". Indonesia, 1990s. $18-20.

Tuki Makeeta Elephant and Ozzie Orangutan. 3.75". Indonesia, 1990s. $18-20.

Cha Cha Frog stacker. 5.5". China, 1990s. $18-20.

Nile Alligator and Cha Cha Frog. 2.75". Indonesia, 1990s. $18-20.

Red Lobster. 4". USA, 1980s. Plastic. Shown in original holder. $6-8.

Red Lobster, Coronita Extra. 8". Mexico, 1990s. Used as table shakers. $6-8.

Rod's Steak House, Williams, Arizona. 3.75". USA, 1950s. Wallace China. $55-60.

Rosie's Diner, Michigan. 2-2.5". USA, 1990s. Jerry Berta. $20-25.

Senor Pico Restaurant, California. 4.25". USA, 1960s. Shown decorated and undecorated. $18-20.

Right:
Sahara Steak House. 4.75". USA, 1960s. Milk glass with plastic tops. $10-12.

Waddles Restaurant, Portland, Oregon. 2.5". Occupied Japan, 1940s. $125-135.

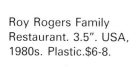

Roy Rogers Family Restaurant. 3.5". USA, 1980s. Plastic.$6-8.

Stuart Anderson's Restaurant, California. 3.5". USA, 1990s. Glass with plastic tops. $6-8.

Right:
Reeb's Restaurant, Porgy and Bess. 5.25". USA, © 1950s. $150-160.

South of the Border, South Carolina. 3.25". Japan, 1950s. PY. $25-30.

Smokquee. The Royal, Boise, Idaho. 3.75". Japan, 1960s. $150-160.

Shoney's Seasoning Salt. 4". USA, 1970s. Plastic. $6-8.

Wagon Wheel, Rockton, Illinois. 3.75". USA, 1950s. $6-8.

White Coffee Pot Restaurants. 3.25". USA, 1950s. Glass with plastic tops. $8-10.

Left and above:
Mr. Bali Hai. 3.5". Japan. 1950s. Made exclusively for the Bali Hai Restaurant, San Diego, California. Shown with jar. Shakers, $20-25.

Tiki Bob's, San Francisco. 4". Japan, 1950s. $12-15.

Trader Vic's. 4.75". USA, 1950s. $12-15.

Ron Clark's Polynesian Village. 4.75". Japan, 1950s. $12-15.

Tiki, Hawaii Kai. 4". Japan, 1960s. Otagiri. $12-15.

Tiki, Kahiki Supper Club, Columbus, Ohio. 4.25". Japan, 1950s. $12-15.

94

Happy Eater. 3". England, 1980s. $10-12.

Happy Eater. 2.25". England, 1980s. $8-10.

Mitchell & Butler's Pub chain, England. 4.5". England, 1980s. Wade. Not sold to the public. $25-30.

Little Chef. 3". England, 1980s. $8-10.

Restaurant in Japan. 4". Japan, 1980s. $8-10.

Churrasacaria Jardim. Rua Republica de Peru. Copacabana. 3.5". Brazil, 1960s. Plastic. $12-15.

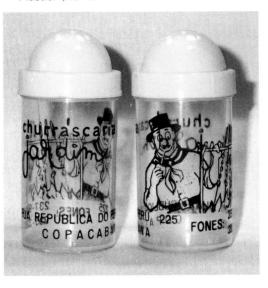

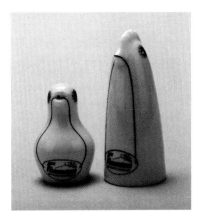

Penang Club, founded 1868. 2.75". England, 1960s. Royal Doulton. $15-18.

Frognerseteren Restaurant. 3.5". Denmark, 1980s. $15-18

Sheraton, Excelsior and Niagara Falls Bell-hops. 4.75". Goebel, Germany, 1950s. Original suitcase straps are leather. $125-135.

HOTELS

Caesars Palace, Las Vegas. 3.5". China, 1990s. $8-10.

Caesars, Atlantic City, NJ. 2". USA, 1990s. $8-10.

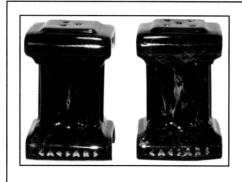

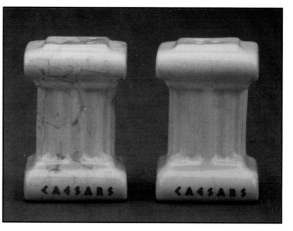

Caesars. 2.25". China, 1990s. $10-12.

Caesars Pocono Resort. 3". China, 1990s. $8-10.

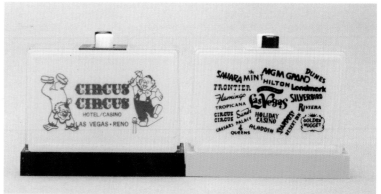

Las Vegas Casinos. 2.5". USA, 1950s. One-piece plastic set. $6-8.

The Story of the Nugget's

Gold Rooster

It was May 1958. The Nugget was preparing to open a new restaurant — the Golden Rooster Room. But one question remained unanswered: what could be done to give specific identity to the new facility. The Nugget's other dining rooms had their own insignia, themes and menus — and so should it be for the Golden Rooster Room.

Management scheduled a "think tank" session and an idea was soon born: make a solid gold statue of a rooster, regal and beautiful — one that could be classified as a masterpiece of art, one that could be displayed and admired by all Nugget guests.

Permission was quickly granted by the San Francisco Mint to make the Golden Rooster. Newman's Silver Shop of Reno and Shreve's of San Francisco were commissioned to fashion the objet d'art from a model created by sculptor-artist Frank Polk.

Within four months the 18-karat gold statue was completed, transported under guard to Reno, and placed in a custom-made glass case near the entrance to the Golden Rooster Room. The beauty of the sculpture, the uniqueness of the work, its value as precious metal — all combined to give the Rooster immediate status as a "must see" attraction for local residents as well as tourists.

Seven months after being on exhibit, the Golden Rooster attracted the attention of the United States Treasury Department, with officials charging that the Nugget was in violation of the Gold Reserve Act which makes it unlawful for a private individual to have more than 50 ounces of gold in his possession unless it is in the form of an object of art.

The Rooster would have to be confiscated.

The Nugget pleaded its case, informing Treasury representatives that permission had been granted through Shreve's by the U.S. Mint. Following verification of the facts by the Treasury, the matter was dropped — for 18 months.

In July 1960 the Nugget was again visited by officers of the Treasury — this time to present the Nugget with a complaint entitled "United States of America vs. One Solid Gold Object in the Form of a Rooster." The Rooster was confiscated and would have to go to jail. The Nugget's attempt to "put up bail" was denied.

After "serving" two years, and after two trial postponements, the Golden Rooster was to have his day in court. The decision would center on one question: was the Golden Rooster an object of art. The Nugget contended the Rooster was a customary and artistic use of gold. The Government disagreed.

At a jury trial in March 1962 the Government was unable to sway the testimony of art critics — all of whom agreed with the Nugget. And so did the jury of ten men and two women.

The Golden Rooster was freed.

And newspapers and wire services throughout the nation carried the story. News headlines shouted: "Solid Gold Bird Liberated."

Amid much display of public approval, the Golden Rooster was returned to the Nugget and its special perch at the entrance to the Golden Rooster Room.

In 1987, when workmen began dismantling the Golden Rooster Room to provide space for a new and enlarged Trader Dick's Restaurant and Lounge, the Rooster was again placed "under wraps" in a secured vault to await another decision: where best could it be returned for public display.

With the completion of the Nugget's new hotel lobby and convention center, the answer was obvious.

In its new and present location in the hotel lobby, the Golden Rooster is readily visible to all Nugget guests — and again the gold statue is the center of attention.

GOLDEN ROOSTER
VITAL STATISTICS

Artistic Value Appraisal in October 1988: $61,784
Height: 9.5 inches
Weight: 206.3 troy ounces (14.1 avoirdupois pounds)
Insured for $140,000
18-Karat Solid Gold

TB-3561-11/92-10M

Left and below:
The Nugget's Golden Rooster, Sparks, NV.
4.25". Japan. $45-50.

Excalibur, Las Vegas. 2". Korea, 1980s. $10-12.

Club Rio, Las Vegas. 5.25". China, 1990s. $18-20.

Excalibur. 2". Korea, 1980s. $10-12.

Excalibur. 2.5". China, 1990s. $10-12.

Harolds Club, Reno. 3.5". USA, 1960s. Glass. $6-8.

Grand Hotel, Butte, Montana. 4". USA, 1950s. One-piece plastic set. $6-8.

Golden Nugget Casino, Las Vegas. 4". Japan, 1960s. $6-8.

Imperial Palace, Las Vegas. 1.75". Korea, 1980s. $10-12.

Right: Flamingo Hilton Hotel/Casino, Las Vegas. 3". China, 1990s. 50th Anniversary. Lotus. $18-20.

Flamingo Hilton. 2.75". China, 1990s. $ 8-10.

Little Joe, Nevada Casino. 4". Probably Japan, 1950s. $12-15.

Flamingo Hilton. 2.5". China, 1990s. $8-10.

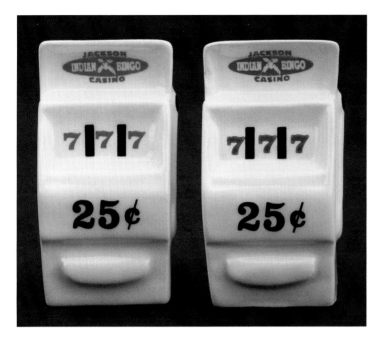

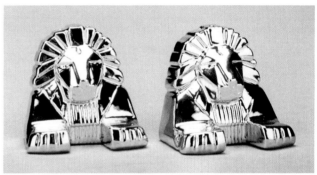

Mandalay Bay, Las Vegas. 2.5". China, 1990s. $10-12.

Jackson Indian Bingo Casino. 3.5". USA, 1990s. $6-8.

Right:
MGM Grand Hotel/
Casino, Las Vegas.
Golden Lion. 2.5".
Taiwan, 1990s.
$25-28.

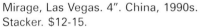

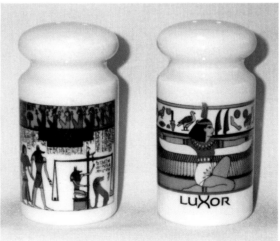

Luxor. 3". China, 1990s.
$10-12.

Mirage, Las Vegas. 4". China, 1990s.
Stacker. $12-15.

Luxor, Las Vegas. 2.5-3".
China, 1990s. $8-10.

Luxor. 2.5". China, 1990s. $10-12.

Left:
Luxor. 2.5". China, 1990s. $10-12.

Harveys Resort Hotel/Casino,
Lake Tahoe, CA. 14.5". USA, New
Year's Eve 1988. $18-20.

Dick Graves Nugget, Sparks,
Nevada. 3.5-4.25" Japan, 1960s.
$35-40.

The Reef Hotel, Waikiki. 3.75".
USA, 1950s. Wood and metal.
$8-10.

Palace Station Hotel/Casino, Las
Vegas. 3.25". China, 1990s. $6-8.

River Side Resort Hotel/
Casino, Laughlin, Nevada.
3.75". Japan, 1980s. Don
Laughlin's. $8-10.

Resorts International Casino, Atlantic City. 2". USA, 1990s. $6-8.

Hotel San Remo Casino/Resort, Las Vegas. 3.5". China, 1990s. $10-12.

Sands Hotel/Casino, Atlantic City. 2". USA, 1990s. $8-10.

Tropicana, Las Vegas. 3.5". China, 1990s. $12-15.

Silver Dollar City, Nevada. 3.5". Japan, 1960s. $10-12.

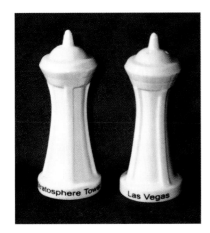

Stratosphere Tower, Las Vegas. 3.5". China, 1990s. $12-15.

Stratosphere. 3". China, 1990s. $10-12.

State Line Smith Casino/Resort, Wendover, Nevada. 2.5". Korea, 1980s. $8-10.

Left set, Hotel Russia, Moscow, 2.5". Right set, Hotel Leningrad. 1.75". Russia. 1960s. $20-25.

The Venetian, Las Vegas. 2.75". China, 1990s. $10-12.

Bellevue Strand Hotel. 3.75". Denmark, 1960s. $12-15.

Hotel Hong Kong. 4". Japan, 1950s. $12-15.

Hotel Australia. 2.5". Denmark, 1950s. Bing & Grondahl. $20-25.

Right and far right: Hotel Australia, Adelaide. 7.5". 1950s. Shown is a close-up of the label. $12-15.

RETAIL STORES

Cabela's Outfitter. 3.5". USA, 1990s. Redwing Pottery. $25-30.

Fingerhut. 2". China, 1990s. $10-12.

Big Dog Sportswear. 4.5". China, 1990s. $18-20.

Eddie Bauer. 2.5". Japan, 1990s. $18-20.

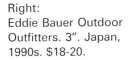

Fort Worth Stockyards. 2". China, 1990s. $6-8.

Left:
Gennings Dry Goods, Gennings, Kansas. 4". USA, 1960s. One-piece plastic set. $8-10.

Right:
Eddie Bauer Outdoor Outfitters. 3". Japan, 1990s. $18-20.

Harrods,
London,
England.
Doorman. 4.25".
England, 1990s.
Wade. $40-45.

Harrods S&P Mill Gift Set. 5.5". England, 1990s.
$20-25.

Left:
Harrods. 4.25".
China, 1990s.
150th anniversary.
$30-35.

Neiman-Marcus hatboxes. 1.75". Taiwan, 1980s. $90-100.

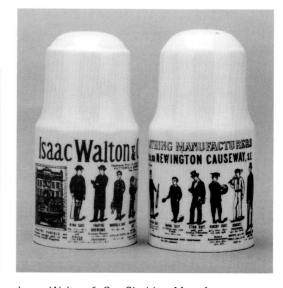

Isaac Walton & Co. Clothing Manufacturers.
4.25". England, 1980s. $12-15.

Left:
Neiman-Marcus.
3". Italy, 1990s.
Silverplate.
$20-25.

Right:
McMahans
Department Store,
Los Angeles,
California. 3.5".
Japan, 1950s.
Christmas give-
aways. $50-55.

Santa's Workshop, North Pole, NY. 3". Japan, 1960s. $12-15.

Santa's Workshop. 1.25". Japan, 1960s. Metal. $10-12.

Wall Drug, South Dakota. 1.5". China, 1990s. $6-8.

Wall Drug. 2.5". China, 1990s. $6-8.

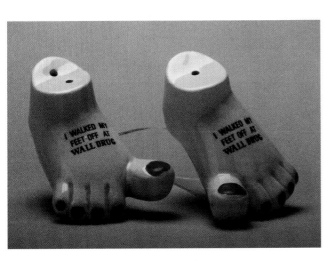

Wall Drug. 1.5". Japan, 1980s. $6-8.

Wall Drug. 3.25". Japan, 1950s. $8-10.

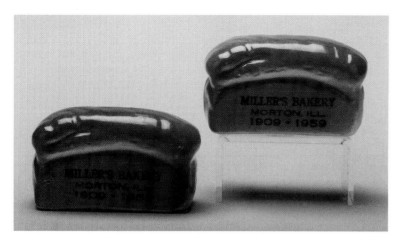

Miller's Bakery, Morton, Illinois. 1.75". USA, 1950s. 50th Anniversary. Morton Pottery. $35-40.

Harry's Cheese House, Wisconsin. 4.25". USA, 1960s. Private Ceramicist. $15-18.

Knott's Berry Farm, California. 3.5". China, 1990s. $8-10.

Above right:
J.B. Bayless Grocery Co. Country Store, Phoenix, Arizona. 3". Japan, 1950s. $18-20.
Far left:
Piggly Wiggly. 3". Japan, 1950s. A grocery chain. $12-15.
Left:
Guadalupe Fish Market, Guadalupe, California. 3.25". Japan, 1950s. $8-10.

Right:
The Mustard Shop, Bridewell Alley, Norwich. 3". England, 1980s. $15-18.

Far right:
Honey Bear Farm. 3.5". Japan, 1980s. "Visit us, Power Lake, Wisconsin." $8-10.

King Pin Foods. 4.5". USA, 1950s.
Rosemeade Pottery. $500+.

Left:
Publix Super Market. 4.5". China, 1990s.
Used in television ads for the store. $12-15.

Perry's Nut House, New England. 2.5".
USA, 1950s. Plastic. $12-15.

Perry's Nut House. 2.5". Japan, 1950s. $125-135.

Risser's Farm Market, Akron, Pennsylvania. 3.5".
USA, 1950s. One-piece plastic set shown with
original sleeve. $6-8.

Mallory Market, Key West, Florida. 2.75". China,
1990s. $6-8.

Thompson's Dairy, CW Deitz Milk and Cream, Muller's Dairy. 3.25".
USA, 1950s. $18-20.

Embassy Fairfax Dairy. 3.25". USA, 1950s. $20-25.

Left:
Green's Milk and Ice Cream. 4". USA, 1950s. One-piece plastic set. $8-10.

Right:
Sealtest National Dairy Products Corp., Warminster Farms Dairies, Sealtest, Single Guernsey Co-Operative. 3.25". USA, 1950s. $18-20.

Slate Belt Dairy, Nelson's Dairies, and Burwick
Creamery. 3.25". USA, 1950s. $18-20.

Clewell's Creamery. 3.25". USA, 1950s. $18-20.

Rose Lawn Milk. 2.25". USA, 1950s.
Glass with metal tops. $8-10.

St Lawrence, East End Dairy, Crystal Creamery Co. 3.25". USA, 1950s. $18-20.

Highland Park
Dairy. 3.25". USA,
1950s. $18-20.

Marigold Rich Milk. 3.25". USA, 1950s. $18-20.

A Fair Shake From Princeton
Dairy. 3". Japan, 1950s. $20-22.

Norges Melk. 1.25". Oslo,
Norway. 1960s. $6-8.

Diederich Dairy. 3.25". USA, 1950s. $18-20.

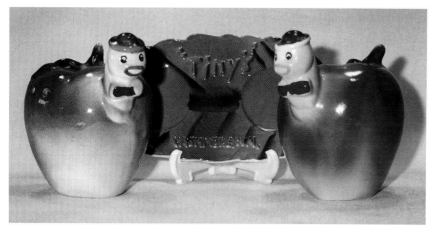

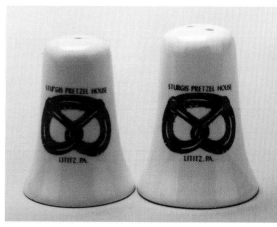

Tiny's Orchard, Cashmere, Minnesota. 3.25". Japan, 1950s. $20-25.

Sturgis Pretzel House, Lititz, Pennsylvania. 2.75". USA, 1980s. $8-10.

Howard L. Butts Shoes. 1.5". USA, 1950s. Glass and metal. $6-8.

Kennedy & Cohen Appliance Store, Florida. 3". Hong Kong, 1960s. Plastic. $10-12.

The Ohio Sample Furniture Co. 3.25". Japan, 1940s. Single $8-10.

Fargo Forum Shoe Store, Fargo, ND. 2.5". USA, 1950s. Rosemeade Pottery. Giveaway shakers from the store. $600+.

Red Goose Shoes. 1.75". USA, 1950s. Metal. $6-8.

Charm Craft Greeting Cards. 3". USA, 1950s. A premium earned for sales. "The beautiful way to remember the day". $12-15.

Left: Clean Gene. Bio-Clean. JADCO. 3". USA, 1970s. Private Ceramicist. 25 sets made. $30-35.

GLASS & PLASTIC COMPANIES

Glenshaw Glass Company Inc. 5.5".
USA, 1995. 100th Anniversary. $15-18.

Glenshaw Glass. 5.75". USA, 1970s. $15-18.

Brockway Glass. 4". USA, 1950s. $10-12.

Knox Glass Inc, Knox, PA. 4".
USA, 1950s. Glass with metal
tops. $8-10.

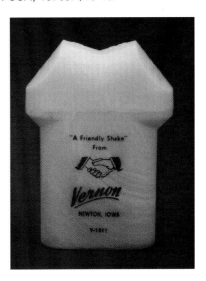

Vernon Plastics. 3.25". USA, 1950s.
One-piece plastic set. $10-12.

Vernon Plastics,
Newton, IA. 2".
USA, 1950s.
One-piece
plastic set.
$8-10.

Oil City Glass Co, Oil City,
Pennsylvania. 2.75". USA, 1950s.
Glass with metal tops. $8-10.

Newton Mfg. Co., Newton, Iowa. 4.5".
USA, 1950s. Glass with plastic tops.
$10-12.

Happy Homer, Staggs-Bilt Homes. Phoenix, Arizona. 4". Japan, 1950s. 1,000 sets made. Happy Homer gave them away only to people who had homes built. $225+.

Above three photos:
Badger Fire Equipment. 4-5.5". USA, 1970s. Possibly sold as mix and match. $18-20/set.

Following three photos:
Stone Electric and Heating. Waterbury Furnaces, Bowman, North Dakota. 2.75". USA, 1950s. Messer Pottery. One-piece set. End, side and opposite end views. $350-375.

Lennie Lennox. Lennox Furnace Co. 4". USA.
One-piece plastic set. $45-50.

Lennie Lennox. 4.75". Probably Japan. ©1950 Lennox Furnace
Co. $100-110.

Lennie Lennox. 4.5". Japan, 1950s. $90-100.

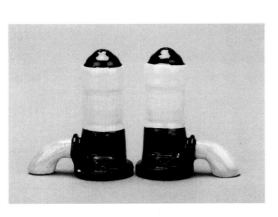

Anderson Pump Co., Chowchilla,
California. 3.5". USA. 1950s. $40-45.

Lennie Lennox. 4.75". USA. © 1950 Lennox Furnace Co.
Composition-like material. $90-100.

SERVICE COMPANIES

Carda Service, Wagner, South Dakota. 4.5". USA, 1950s. $18-20.

Falls Creek Baptist Assembly, Davis, Oklahoma. 3.25". USA, 1960s. One-piece plastic set. $8-10.

North American Van Lines. 2.5". USA, 1970s. $10-12.

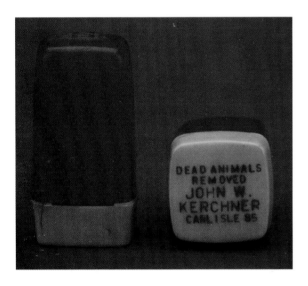

Left:
Dead Animals Removed. John W. Kerchner, Carlisle 85, Pennsylvania. 1.75". USA, 1950s. $6-8.

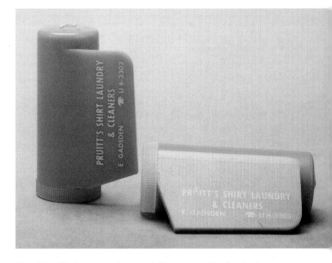

Pruitt's Shirt Laundry and Cleaners, E. Gadsden, Alabama. 2.5". USA, 1950s. Plastic. $6-8.

Right:
Perala Funeral Home, Negaunee, Michigan. "A Fair Shake ALL-WAYS." 3.75". USA, 1950s. Glass with metal tops. $10-12.

Far right:
Laughter-North Funeral Home. 4". USA, 1950s. One-piece plastic set. "Seasonings Greetings". $8-10.

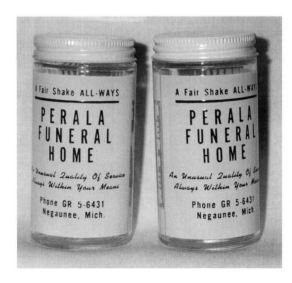

ELECTRIC COMPANIES

Southwest Electric Co-Op, Missouri. 3.75".
USA, 1960s. One-piece plastic set. $8-10.

Top right:
Ozark Electric Co-Op. 3.5".
USA, 1960s. Plastic. $6-8.

Right:
Redi-Kilowatt. 3.5". USA,
1950s. Plastic. $12-15.

Westinghouse Electric Ranges. "The
Taste Makers". 2.5". USA, 1960s. One-
piece plastic set. $6-8.

Medallion Home. "Live
Better Electrically". 2".
USA, 1950s. Plastic.
$6-8.

Left:
First Electric Coop-
erative Corp. 2".
USA, 1950s. Plastic.
$6-8.

Right:
"Live Better Electri-
cally". 2". USA,
1950s. Plastic. $6-8.

GAS COMPANIES

Canadian Gas Genies. 4". Japan, 1970s. $75-80.

Handy Flame. Citizen's Gas Co., Indianapolis, Indiana. 4.25". USA, 1950s. $12-15.

Handy Flame. 3.5-3.75". Japan, 1950s. $12-15.

Skelgas. 5". USA, 1950s. One-piece plastic set. Shown with original sleeve. $10-12.

Speedy Flame and Thrifty Flame Gas companies. 4.5". USA, 1950s. $18-20.

Ideal Gas Co. 2.5". USA, 1950s. $15-18.

Phillip's Bottled Gas, E. Toledo, Ohio. 3". USA, 1950s. Plastic. $6-8.

Three different gas companies. 2.75". USA, 1950s. Plastic. $6-8.

Pyrofax Gas. 3.75". USA, 1960s. Plastic. $10-12.

Tempo Co-Op. 3". Canada, 1990s. $8-10.

Left:
Flame Gas Co. 2". USA, 1950s. Plastic. $6-8.

Pyrane Bottled Gas. 4.75". USA, 1960s. $8-10.

Philgas. 1.75". USA, 1950s. Plastic. $6-8.

Yellow Pages. 3.75". USA, 1970s. One-piece plastic set. $8-10.

Bell Telephone. 4". USA, 1980s. Give-aways to company employees. $10-12.

FINANCIAL INSTITUTIONS

First Bank of Tulsa, Oklahoma. 2.5". USA, 1950s. Frankoma Pottery. Given away during grand opening. $40-45.

Fruita State Bank, Colorado. 2.75". USA, 1950s. $12-15.

Minneapolis Savings & Loan Association. 3.75". USA, 1980s. Plastic. "A Good Time to Come to Us for Shelter". $12-15.

B&O Chessie Employees Federal Credit Union. 3.5". USA, 1970s. Plastic. $6-8.

Exchange State Bank, Lanark, Illinois. 3.5". USA, 1960s. Plastic. $6-8.

Harris Bank, Illinois. 4". Japan, 1970s. $20-25.

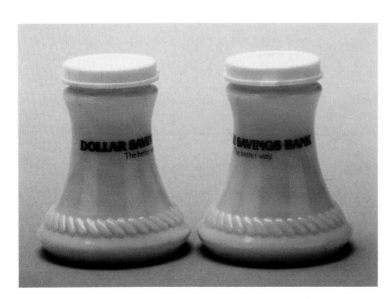

Dai-Ichi Life. 3.25". Japan, 1990s. ©Walt Disney. $125-135.

Dollar Savings Bank. 2.5". USA, 1960s. Glass with plastic tops. $8-10.

Amicable Life Insurance Company, Waco, Texas. 4". USA, 1970s. Glass with plastic tops. $8-10.

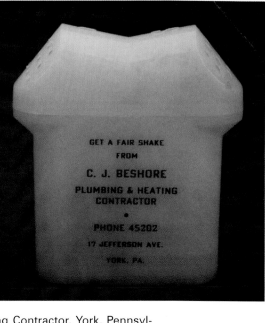

Roto Rooter Sewer Service. 3.75".
USA, 1960s. One-piece plastic set.
$10-12.

C.J.Beshore Plumbing and Heating Contractor, York, Pennsylvania. 3.25-4". USA, 1960s. One-piece plastic set. $8-10.

Red Cross Pharmacy, Overton,
Nebraska. 2.25". USA, 1950s.
Metal. $6-8.

Salvation Army. 2". England, 1950s.
Metal. $8-10.

Deutsches Roteskruez (German
Red Cross). 3.5". Germany,
1990s. $8-10.

US Postal Service. 3". Korea,
1980s. Ron Gordon Designs,
New Jersey. $10-12.

UPS Driver and Truck. 4.75". USA, 1950s. One-
piece plastic set. $20-25.

UAW Local 594, GMC Truck and
Bus, Pontiac, Michigan. 3.5". USA,
1970s. Milk Glass. $8-10.

120

HOUSEHOLD

APPLIANCES

Admiral, Smith's Home Furnishings, Hinton, Oklahoma. 2.5". USA, 1960s. One-piece plastic set. $8-10.

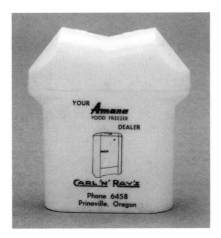

Amana Food Freezer. Carl-N-Ray's, Prineville, Oregon. 4". USA, 1950s. One-piece plastic set. $8-10.

Admiral Refrigerators and TV, Ramsey Machinery Co., Plains, Kansas. 3.75". USA, 1950s. One-piece plastic set. $8-10.

Right:
Eveready. 2.5".
Hong Kong,
1970s. Metal.
$8-10.

Right three photos:
Compact Vacuum Cleaners.
1.5". USA, 1960s. Plastic.
$10-12.

Above and right:
Kelvinator. 3.75".
USA, 1950s. One-
piece plastic set with
four sections. $12-15.

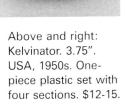

Filter Queen Vacuum Cleaners. 2″. USA, 1950s. Plastic. $15-18.

Filter Queen shown in original package. $20-22.

General Electric Refrigerators with Sugar Bowl or Grease Holder. Shakers 3".
USA, 1950s. Milk glass with metal tops. Note: right set has indented GE labels.
Shakers, $25-30. Complete set, $45-50.

Starmix Blender. 3.75". USA,
1950s. Plastic. $18-20.

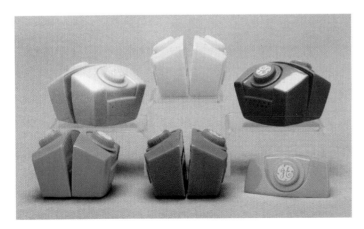

General Electric Sleep Guard Blankets. 1.25". USA, 1950s.
Plastic. $15-18.

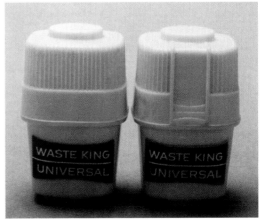

Waste King Universal (Garbage Disposal). 3".
USA, 1950s. Plastic. $20-25.

Kenmore Toaster. 4". Japan. ©1986 Beetland. Metal with ceramic toast. $85-90.

Sears Washer & Dryer. 2.5". Hong Kong. 1960s. One-piece plastic snow-dome set. $45-50.

Left:
Magic Chef. 5.75". USA, 1970s. Private Ceramicist. $25-30.

Magic Chef. 5-5.25". USA, 1960s. Left set, ceramic, $45-50. Right set, plastic, $30-35.

Magic Chef. 3.5". USA, 1950s. Milk glass with plastic tops. $25-30.

Tappan. 4". USA, 1950s. Glass. $18-20.

Tappan. 4". Japan, 1960s. $18-20.

WESTINGHOUSE: AMERICA'S FAVORITE LAUNDRY TWINS
3-3.25". USA, 1960s.

Above two photos:
Philco Refrigerator. 4.25". USA, 1950s. Glass with metal tops, shown in original sleeve. $15-18.

Without back panel. $10-12.

Coleman Lanterns. 2". Hong Kong, 1960s. $20-22.

With slanted rear panel. Shown with original package. $20-25.

With back panel and no buttons. $12-15.

With back panel and buttons. $15-18.

With back panel and no buttons. One shown in original package. $15-18.

With raised back panel and buttons, in original package. $18-20.

OTHER

Nicholas Laboratories Ltd. Antacid. 4.5".
England, 1982. $30-35.

Asilone Protects. Antacid. 3.5".
England, 1980s. $30-35.

Speedy Alka Seltzer. 5.75". USA, 1990s.
Private ceramicist. Unlicensed. $50-55.

Right:
Coricidin. 3.5". England,
1990s. $25-30.

Mary Kay Cosmetics. 1.5". USA, 1990s. $20-25

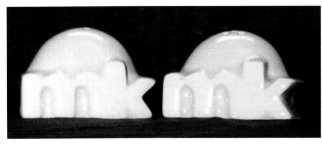

Right:
Coppertone Boy and
Girl. 4". Japan, 1960s.
Unlicensed. $185-200.

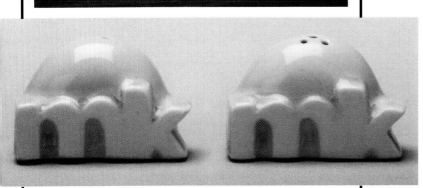

My Merry Foot Powder/Talc. 1.5".
USA, 1950s. Cardboard. $6-8.

Gleem Toothpaste. 2-3.5". Japan, 1950s. Left set, plastic. Right set, wood. $6-8.

Left two photos:
Proctor & Gamble Ivory
Soap. 2". USA, 1940s. Front
and back views. One-piece
chalkware set. $22-25.

Le Gui (Mistletoe) Sachet/Talc, Portland,
Oregon. 2". USA, 1950s. Plastic. $6-8.

Pears Soap. 4". England,
1980s. $12-15.

Van Houten's Cocoa and Brooke's Soap.
Singles. 4". England, 1980s. $6-8 each.

Ball Mason Jars. 4". USA, 1980s. Shown in original box. $6-8.

Drey Mason Jars. 3.75". USA, 1950s. $20-25.

Ball Mason Jars. 2.75". USA, 1960s. Glass with metal tops. $6-8.

Jewel Tea Company Stove. 5". USA, 1950s. Metal with glass shakers. $18-20.

Ball Mason Jars. 2.75". USA, 1930s. Zinc tops. $18-20.

Left:
Mautz Paint. 1.5". USA, 1960s. Cardboard. $6-8 pair.

General Electric. 3.5". USA, 1960s. Shown with original package. $6-8.

Left:
Gleem Paints. 1.5". USA, 1960s. Plastic. $6-8.

Left:
Camel Cigarettes, Max & Ray. 3.5-4". China. © 1993 RJRTC. Left set, plastic, $10-12. Right set, ceramic, $15-18.

Right:
Philadelphia Phillies. 4". USA, 1950s. Wood. $8-10.

Kool Cigarettes. Millie and Willie. 3.5". Left set, USA, 1950s. F&F Mold and Die Works, plastic, $10-12. Right set, Taiwan, 1990s. Ceramic reproduction, $6-8.

Left:
Ken-L-Ration, Fifi and Fido. 3.25". USA, 1950s. F & F Mold & Die Works. $10-12.

Admiration Cigars. 2.75". Japan, 1950s. Shown with original box. $45-50.

Dog Shampoo. 3". USA, 1970s. Plastic. Pharma Craft Corp. $6-8.

Ely Dog Biscuits. 4.25". USA, 1960s. $20-22.

ENTERTAINMENT

TELEVISION

Bride and Groom Show, Hollywood. 4.25". USA, 1950s. Also comes as a redhead. $12-15.

Nick at Nite Classic TV. 5.5". China, 1997. ©Viacom. $30-35.

"I Love Lucy" shoes. 2". China, 1990s. Vandor. $15-18.

Left:
Happy Days. 4.5". China, 1990s. ©Viacom. Glass with metal tops. $18-20.

Ricky Ricardo's Club Babalu, "I Love Lucy". 3.25". China. ©1997. Dist. by Viacom. $20-22.

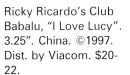

RCA Corp. 3.25-3.5". USA, 1950s. Left set, Lenox $25-30. Right set, copy, $20-22.

Tower Records. 3". USA, 1990s. $6-8.

RCA Corp. 3-3.5". USA, 1950s. $20-22.

SS Love Boat. 1.75". Japan, 1979. Enesco. $12-15.

RCA Corp. Nipper. 3". Left set, Japan, $12-15. Right set, USA, 1980s, Plastic, $10-12.

Wurlitzer stacker. 3.5". China. ©1998 Wurlitzer Jukebox Co. $12-15.

Right and far right: WMBR Radio Station, Jacksonville, Florida. 4". USA, 1960s. One-piece plastic set. $8-10.

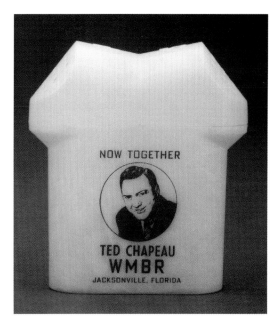

WGN Chicago Radio and Television Stations. 3.5". USA, 1960s. $8-10.

Billy Bob's, Fort Worth, Texas. 1.5-3.5". China, 1990s. $6-8/set.

McGuffey's Reader. 3.5". Japan, 1960s. $8-10.

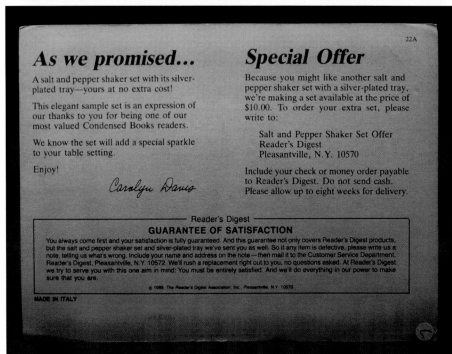

Captain Bob-Lo Amusement Park, near Detroit. 5". Japan, 1950s. $70-75.

Reader's Digest. 1.75". Italy, 1980s. Front and back views. $8-10.

The Salt Jumper & the Pepper Jumper. 3.75". USA, 1970s. Private ceramicist. Left shaker, "For World's Record, read 'The Big Flight' at your library or order direct." Right shaker, "This event was accomplished by Kevin Seaman 1-18-76 at Ski-Hi Pioneer DZ, Phoenix, AZ." $18-20.

Lego. 3.25". USA. 1990s. Plastic. $12-15.

MOVIES

WIZARD OF OZ

Good Witch and Wicked Witch. 3.75".
Philippines, 1990s. Clay Art. $18-20.

Dorothy & Scarecrow and Tin Man &
Cowardly Lion. 3.5" Philippines,
1990s. Clay Art. $18-20.

Dorothy and Cowardly Lion.
5". China, 1990s. ©TEC. Star
Jars. $15-18.

Tin Man and Scarecrow. 5.25". China,
1990s. ©TEC. Star Jars. $15-18.

Ruby Slippers. 2". China, 1990s.
©TEC98. Star Jars. $15-18.

Scarecrow. 4". China, 1990s. ©99
TEC. Enesco. $12-15.

Wicked Witch. 4.5". China, 1990s.
©99 TEC. Enesco. $12-15.

Cowardly Lion. 4". China, 1990s. ©99
TEC. Enesco. $12-15.

Dorothy & The Talking Tree. 5". China, 1990s. ©TEC 99. Judy Garland as Dorothy. $25-30.

Dorothy & Toto. 4.25". China. ©WB 97. Judy Garland as Dorothy. $25-30.

Tin Man & Heart. 4.5". China, 1990s. ©WB 98. As portrayed by Jack Haley. $25-30.

Ruby Slippers. 2". China, 1990s. ©WB 97. $25-30.

Witches' Hats. 3.5". China, 1990s. ©WB 98. $25-30.

Left:
Munchkin Mayor. 4.25". China, 1990s. ©WB 98. $25-30.

These S&Ps made by Star jars for OZ chess-board cookie jar. Complete series: 1 Cookie Jar, eight pawn sets, two rook sets, one set each of other six S&Ps. Also sold separately, $25-35 each.

Wizard of Oz & Evil Wizard, Kings
Emerald City & Witch's Castle, Rooks

Cowardly Lion & Winged Monkey, Knights
Scarecrow & Winged Monkey, Knights

Left:
Tin Man & Witch's
Soldier, Bishops
Glinda (Good Witch) &
Witch's Soldier, Bishops

Right:
Dorothy & Wicked Witch,
Queens
Ruby Slippers & Witch's
Hat, Pawns

Below:
Toy Story Buzz & Woody.
6". China, 1990s.
Treasure Craft. $35-40.

Toy Story Alien. 3.5". Japan, 1990s. ©Disney. Made for
Japanese market. $45-50.

137

Babe. 3.75". China, 1990s. TM & © Universal Studios. $20-25.

The Harvey Girls (from the movie of the same name). 3.5". Japan, 1950s. $75-80.

Gone With the Wind. Rhett Butler & Scarlett O'Hara. 4.5". China, 1990s. CTM TEC & SMT (Steven Mitchell Trusts) 99. $35-40.

Gone With the Wind. 5". USA, 1990s. Rick Wisecarver, Ohio. $50-55.

Backdraft. (From the movie of the same name). 2.25". China, 1990s. Copyright 1991 UCS & IFE. $50-55.

Titanic. 2.5". China, 1990s. Enesco. $12-15.

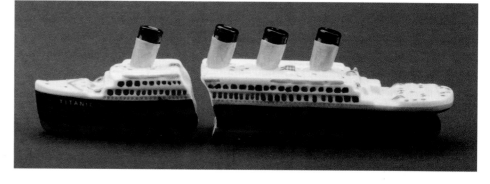

Earthquake. 2.25". Taiwan, 1990s. "I survived earthquake at Universal Studios". $8-10.

Streetcar Named Desire. 1.75". Japan, 1950s. $8-10.

SPORTS

Right and far right: Cumberland Drive-In Theater & Midway Bowling Center. 4". USA, 1950s. One-piece plastic set with advertising on each side. $8-10.

"For Fun and Relaxation"
CUMBERLAND DRIVE-IN THEATRE
Midway Between Carlisle and Shippensburg On Route 11

"For Fun and Relaxation"
MIDWAY BOWLING CENTER
Midway Between Carlisle and Mt. Holly Springs On Route 34 Phone CH 9-1222

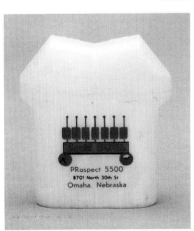

Left:
Kelley's North Bowl, Omaha, Nebraska. 4". USA. 1950s. One-piece plastic set. $8-10.

Right:
Dunlop. 1.75". England, 1980s. $15-18.

Calgary Flames. 1.5". Taiwan, 1990s. Gift Craft. $10-12.

Les Canadiens, Montreal. 1.5". Taiwan, 1990s. $10-12.

National Football League Tasmanian Devil. 3.5". China, 1990s. Shown is New England Patriots. Twelve other teams pictured in "1003 Salt and Pepper Shakers". $18-20.

Go Big Red, No. 1 Nebraska National Champs '70 & '71. 3.5". USA, 1980s. Plastic. $8-10.

NBA Basketball. 3". China, 1990s. Shown are Chicago Bulls. Other teams also made. $12-15.

Green Bay Packers. 2.5". China, 1990s. $8-10.

Jasper Bears (A Canadian Campground). 3.75". Canada, 1980s. $30-35.

Butler's Red Coats, Holiday Camps. 3.75". England, 1980s. $30-35.

Atlanta Braves & Chicago
Cubs. 4.5" China, 1990s.
©MLB 1998. $25-30.

Colorado Rockies &
Los Angeles Dodgers.
4.5". China, 1990s.
©MLB 1998. $25-30.

New York Yankees & Saint
Louis Cardinals. 4.5". China,
1990s. © MLB 1998. $25-30.

Left:
Los Angeles Dodgers.
4.25". Japan, 1970s.
$15-18.

Right:
Texas Rangers. 2.5".
USA, 1950s. Compo-
sition material.
$12-15.

Georgia Bulldogs. 4".
China, 1990s. $12-15.

Kansas Jayhawks. 2.5". USA,
1950s. Rosemeade Pottery. $500+.

Kansas Jayhawks. 3.25". USA, 1960s. $30-35.

Kansas Jayhawks Cheerleaders. 2.25". USA, 1950s.
Rosemeade Pottery. $600+.

COLLEGIATE SERIES
4". China. 1990s. $15-18

Alabama Crimson Tide,
Kansas State Wildcats,
Arkansas Razorbacks.

Kansas Jayhawks, Louisiana State Tigers.

University of California,
Berkley Honey Bears,
Georgia Bulldogs, North
Carolina Tarheels.

Florida Seminoles, Indiana Hoosiers.

Tennessee Volunteer Dogs.

Nebraska Cornhuskers, Michigan Wolverines.

Clemson Tigers, North Carolina State Wolfpack, Florida Gators.

Kentucky Wildcats, Louisville Cardinals, Auburn Tigers.

Mississippi State Bulldogs, Virginia Tech Hokies.

Penn State Nittany Lions, South Carolina Gamecocks, Colorado Buffaloes.

BEVERAGES

WINE AND LIQUOR

Left and right:
Blossom Valley Foxes. 5.75". USA, 1960s.
Regal China. ©Dave Nissen. 500 sets
produced. Front and back views. $50-55

Center left:
Blue Nun. 4.25". Japan, 1960s. Composition material. $90-100.

Left and above:
Blue Nun. 7.5". USA,
1950s. Glass with plastic
tops. Note name on tops.
$25-30.

Below left:
Cohovas Vineyards,
Geneva, Ohio. 3.75". USA,
1960s. $12-15.

Below:
Plymouth Martini. 4".
USA, 1960s. $10-12.

Michter's Whiskey, Shaefferstown,
Pennsylvania. 2". USA, 1960s. $12-15.

Dickel Tennessee Whiskey. 4.5". USA, 1960s. $12-15.

Dickel Tennessee. 13". USA, 1950s. "27 years of stubbornness, but we made it". First Bottling, October 1964. $20-25.

Mount Hope Wines, Pennsylvania. 5". USA, 1990s. $10-12.

Sandeman Liqueur.. 5.25". Japan, 1950s. $35-40.

Nikolai Vodka. 4.5". Japan, 1960s. Made for Four Roses Distillers. Co. Dundalk, Maryland. $55-60.

Pusser's of the West Indies (rum), Tortola, British Virgin Islands. 3.5". England, 1980s. Wade. $60-65.

Two Fingers Tequila. 4.25". USA, 1980s. $18-20.

Seagram's 7 Crown. 3.5". USA, 1950s. Plastic. $12-15.

Seagram's Crown Royal. 3.5". Canada, 1980s. $8-10.

Cutty Sark & Dewars Scotch. 5". Scotland, 1970s. $10-12.

Vat 69. 4". England, 1970s. Plastic and ceramic. $35-40.

Vat 69. 4.25". Japan, 1960s. Plastic. $6-8.

Mateus Rose Wine. 3.25". Portugal, 1960s. $25-30.

Suc Froezien Liqueur. Simon-Villard, Roanne, Loire. 3.25". France, 1980s. Single shaker, $18-20.

Wolfschmidt Vodka. S&P, 4.5". Total, 9.75". Japan. Complete set with celery salt, onion salt, and red pepper shakers, $35-40.

Le Piat de Beaujolais. 4.75". France, 1990s. $18-20.

Moet & Chandon Champagne. 2.5". France, 1980s. $20-25.

Marchesi di Barolo, Pepper Mill. 10.5". Italy, 1980s. Close-up of label shown. $15-18.

Scali Chianti. 6". Italy, 1980s. Glass with plastic tops. $6-8.

McWilliams, New Zealand. 3.25". Japan, 1980s. Left set, Moselle. Right set, Semi-sweet Sherry. $25-30.

Seppelt. 4.75". Australia, 1960s. Mischer. $12-15.

Beenleigh Rum, New Zealand. "The Original Bosun of SS Walrus". 3". Japan, 1980s. $15-18.

ATE Kuhlung. 5". Probably from Scandinavia. Single shaker. $10-12.

Black Tower, Liebfraumilch. 5.25". Germany, 1970s. $35-40.

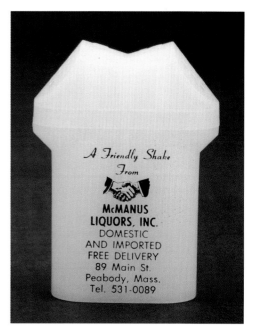

Corrida. "It's never been easier to enjoy good wine". 4". Sweden, 1980s. Scandic Designed Stoneware, Ltd. $15-18.

Babycham Sparkling Perry. 6.25". England, 1980s. $15-18.

McManus Liquors Inc. 3". USA, 1960s. One-piece plastic set. $8-10.

BEER

Ben Truman. 3.75".
England, 1980s.
$20-25.

Right:
Burger Bohemian
Beer. 4". USA, 1950s.
$15-18.

Blatz. 4.25". USA, 1960s. Bottom of ceramic tray marked "Souvenirs and Novelties. Bill's Specialty Mfg. Co., Milwaukee 3 Wis". Glass shakers with metal tops. $15-18.

Blatz Beer. Milwaukee's Finest. 3". USA, 1950s. $12-15.

Ballantine. 2.25". USA, 1960s. Metal. $6-8.

Stroh's Brewery Company Burgie.
4.75". Japan, 1998. Silver State
Specialties, California. $35-40.

Bud Man. 3.5-3.75". Brazil. Ceramarte. Left set, 1960s, $140-150. Right set, 1990s, $15-18.

Six Pack. 2.75". China, 1990s. Enesco. $12-15.

Spuds McKenzie. 3.5". Japan, 1990s. Unlicensed. Five & Dime Inc. $15-18.

Anniversary steins. 3.75". Brazil, 1960s. Ceramarte. $90-100.

4.5". Taiwan, 1990s. $8-10.

3". USA, 1950s. $12-15.

4.5". Salt & pepper mill. USA, 1990s. Plastic and metal. Mr. Dudley. $8-10.

Christmas soccer balls.
3.5". USA, 1990s. $10-12.

Deliveryman and cart. 4". China, 1990s. Enesco prototype. Unpriced.

Stackers. Dalmatian with cases and two-piece stein. 4.25". China, 1990s. Enesco prototypes. Unpriced.

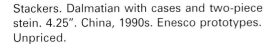

Beer Wagon and Horse. 3". China, 1990s. Enesco prototype. Unpriced.

2.25". USA. 1990s. $8-10.

3.5". Hong Kong, 1980s. Plastic. $4-6.

4.25". Taiwan, 1980s. Plastic. $4-6.

Above four photos:
Anheuser Busch. 3.5". USA, 1990s. $8-10.

Coors. 4". USA, 1980s. $8-10.

Coors Golden Beer. 2-4". USA, 1960s. $25-30.

Coors Golden Beer. 3.5". USA, 1960s. $25-30.

Coors. 2.25". USA, 1950s. One-piece plastic set shown with original box. $10-12.

Drewrys Ale, South Bend, Indiana. 4.25". USA, 1950s. Glass with metal tops. $12-15.

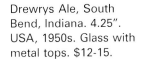

Falstaff. 3". USA, 1950s. $12-15.

Coors. 3.5". USA, 1990s. Plastic and metal. $6-8.

Eastside Beer, Los Angeles Brewing Company. 3". USA, 1950s. $12-15.

Left:
Kirin. 3". Japan, 1970s. Plastic. $8-10.

Leinenkugel's Beer. "Made with Chippewa Water from the Big Eddy Springs". 4". USA, 1960s. $12-15.

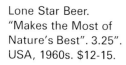

Kloster. 2.25". Mexico, 1950s. Cerveceria Cuauhtemoc. Metal, $10-12.

Koch's Golden Anniversary Beer. 2.25". USA, 1960s. $6-8.

Lone Star Beer, San Antonio, Texas. 3.25". USA, 1970s. ©Loma Products. $15-18.

Lone Star Beer. "Makes the Most of Nature's Best". 3.25". USA, 1960s. $12-15.

Theodore. 3.5". England, 1990s. Wade. 150 sets made with British flag, 350 sets with USA flag. $30-35.

Black Theodore in his teepee. 5.25". Japan, 1990s. Limited edition; 100 made for Hamm's Club members. Standard Hamm's decal. Silver State Specialties. Issue price $49.95.

Theodore in his canoe. 3.25". Japan, 1990s. Limited editions; 100 of each color combination made for Hamm's Club members. Silver State Specialties. Issue price $45.00. Also sold as black bear in brown canoe, 1000 sets produced. Issue price $35.00.

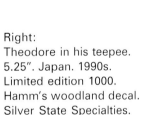

Right:
Theodore in his teepee. 5.25". Japan. 1990s. Limited edition 1000. Hamm's woodland decal. Silver State Specialties. Issue price $39.95.

4.75". Japan, 1997. Silver State Specialties. $30-35.

Original Hamm's Bears. 4.25". Japan, 1960s. $75-80.

4.75". Brazil, 1970s. Ceramarte. $40-45.

4.75". Japan, 1997. Silver State Specialties. $30-35.

Turnabouts. 5.5". USA, 1970s. Private ceramicist. $30-35.

4.75". Japan, 1997. Silver State Specialties. $30-35.

3-3.75". USA, 1950s. Glass with metal tops. $15-18.

3.75". USA, 1950s. Glass with metal tops. Bar salt shakers. $25-30 each.

3.5". USA, 1990s. $8-10.

Miller. 4.5". Taiwan, 1990s. $8-10.

Miller Hi-Life. 7". USA, 1960s. Siesta ware. $8-10.

Pabst. 3". USA, 1950s. $12-15.

Miller. 3". USA, 1950s. $12-15.

Left:
Pabst Blue Ribbon. 4.25". USA, 1950s.
Glass with metal tops. $15-18.

Olympia. 4". USA, 1960s. $25-30.

Olympia. 3.75". Japan, 1990s. $8-10.

Panimooy Bock Vaasa Wasa. 3.25". Scandinavia, 1950s. $8-10.

Left:
Peerless Amber. La Crosse Breweries Inc., Wisconsin. 5". USA, 1960s. $45-50.

Right:
Pearl Lager Beer. "From the Country of 1100 Springs". 3.5". USA, 1960s. $12-15.

Straub. 5.5". USA, 1960s. Glass with metal tops. $8-10.

Burt and Harry Piel. 4". Japan, 1960s. $45-50.

Piels Real Draft. 4". USA, 1950s. Glass with metal tops. $8-10.

Red Dog. 4". Taiwan, 1990s. $8-10.

Stroh's. Stroh's Light. 5.5". Japan, 1990s. Silver State Specialties. Copyright Stroh's Brewery Co. $22-25.

Red Dog. 3". Hong Kong, 1980s. Plastic. $6-8.

Rolling Rock. 7". USA, 1970s. Glass with plastic tops. $8-10.

Stroh's. 7". USA, 1970s. Pewter. Gifts to Stroh's employees. $30-35.

Union Brewery, Virginia City, Nevada. "Jewel of the Comstock". 5". Japan, 1990s. Replica of original beer bottle. $25-30.

Utica Club Schultz and Dooley. 4.25-4.5". Right set, gold top, Brazil, Ceramarte, $100-110. Other sets, Germany. $45-50.

Guinness. 5". England, 1960s. Plastic. $35-40.

Guinness Extra Stout. 4".
England, 1960s. Wood.
$18-20.

Guinness turtles. 3.25". England, 1960s. Carltonware. $150+.

Guinness. 2". England,
1960s. Single promo-
tional shaker. $25-30.

Left:
Guinness. 4.5". Japan,
1960s. 3-piece set.
$100-110.

Right:
Guinness. 5". England,
1970s. Carltonware.
$40-45.

Guinness Extra Stout condiment. 3.5". Japan, 1950s. $120-125.

Guinness toucan condiment. 3.75". England, 1960s. Carltonware. $90-100.

Right:
Guinness condiment. 5". England, 1970s. Plastic. $35-40.

Guinness toucans. 3.75". China, 1960s. $35-40.

Huntsman Ales. "The Beer of Wessex." 2.5". England, 1970s. Burleighware. $25-30.

Jubilee Stout condiment. 3". England, 1970s. Wade. $45-50.

Tennent's Lager. 5". England, 1970s. Wade. $35-40.

Shepherd Neame Master Brewers condiment. 4". England, 1970s. $30-35.

Left:
La Canadienne Beer. Quebec. 4.5". Canada, 1960s. Glass with metal top. $6-8.

Heineken Draught Lager condiment. 5". England, 1970s. Carltonware. $70-75.

Right:
Skol Lager. 4.75". England, 1990s. $18-20.

164

Whitbread Tankard London Beer. 9".
England, 1970s. $18-20.

Tetley condiment. 4.5". England, 1980s. $30-35.

Tetley Bittermen condiment. 2.5".
England, 1980s. Burleighware.
$30-35.

Whitbread Brewers condiment. 3".
England, 1980s. $30-35.

Whitbread condiment. 3". England, 1980s.
$30-35.

Carling's Black Label Beer. 4". USA, 1950s. $12-15.

Canadian Cream Ale, Buffalo, New York. 4.25". USA. 1950s. $15-18.

Lord Camden Beer and Ale, Camden, New Jersey. 4". USA, 1950s. Glass with metal tops. $12-15.

Arrow Beer, Baltimore, Maryland. 4". USA, 1950s. $18-20.

Esslinger, Philadelphia's Premium Beer. 3.75". USA, 1950s. Glass with metal tops. $12-15.

Left:
Grain Belt Beer. 3.75". USA, 1950s. Bar salt shaker. $25-30.

Right:
Old Dutch Beer. Eagle Brewing Co., Catasauqua, Pennsylvania. 3.75". USA, 1950s. $15-18.

Lang's Bohemian Beer. Gerhardt Lang Brewery, Buffalo, New York. 4.25". USA, 1950s. $18-20.

Koppitz Beer, Detroit, Michigan. 3". USA, 1950s. $12-15.

Old Export Beer, Cumberland Brewing Co., Cumberland, Maryland. 4". USA, 1950s. Glass with metal tops. $15-18.

Red Top Ale, Red Top Brewing Co., Cincinnati, Ohio. 4". USA, 1950s. $20-22.

Prager Beer, Atlas Brewing Co., Chicago, Illinois. 3-4.5". USA, 1950s. $10-12.

Schlitz. "The Beer That Made Milwaukee Famous". 2.25". USA, 1950s. Cardboard and metal. $6-8.

Tiptop Bohemian Beer. The Sunrise Brewing Co., Cleveland, Ohio. 3". USA, 1950s. Glass with metal tops. $20-22.

Schaefer Beer, New York, New York. 4-4.25". USA, 1950s. Glass with metal tops. $18-20.

Right:
Trophy Beer, Chicago, Illinois. 3.75". USA, 1950s. Glass with metal tops. $18-20.

Center:
Stein's Canandaigua Beer, Canandaigua, New York. 3.75". USA, 1950s. Glass with metal tops. $18-20.

Far right:
Schoenling Ale, The Schoenling Brewing Co., Cincinnati, Ohio. 7". USA, 1950s. $12-15.

SODA

COCA COLA

3.5". China, 1990s. $12-15.

7.25". China, 1990s. 3 pieces. $15-18.

3.5". China, 1990s. $10-12.

3". China, 1990s. $12-15.

Mini Coke and hot dog. 2.25". USA, 1950s. $35-40.

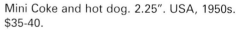

Coca Cola and Hot Dog. 4". Sri Lanka, 1980s. Enesco. $15-18.

2.5". USA, 1960s. Metal. $6-8.

Fountain Service. 4". China, 1990s. Metal. $12-15.

Cooler-style machine. 3". Taiwan, 1990s. Stacker. $15-18.

4". Sri Lanka, 1980s. Ceramic bottles. Enesco. $12-15.

3.25". USA, 1960s. One-piece plastic set. $10-12.

3". Germany, 1990s. Ceramic Coke cans on tray. $20-25.

4". USA, 1960s. One-piece plastic set. $10-12.

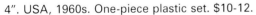

3.25". China, 1990s. Enesco. $12-15.

Coca Cola and Fanta. 3". Chile, 1950s. Plastic three-piece set with pencil holder. Plasticos Inyectados. $20-25.

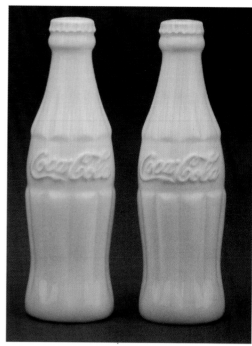

5.5". China, 1990s. $10-12.

Left:
Coca Cola 6-set series in a display case. S&P, 2-4". Display case, 13". China, 1990s. Enesco. ©1996 The Coca Cola Company. Complete set, $100-125.

Right:
5". China, 1990s. Stacker. $10-12.

Victorian Series. 5.25". China, 1990s. Sold exclusively by Cracker Barrel. Shown with original box. $10-12.

Traditional bottles. 5.5". China, 1990s. Sun Belt Marketing. $15-18.

Ceramic bottles with napkin holder. 3.25". Taiwan, 1970s. $15-18.

2.5". USA, 1980s. Glass with metal tops. $8-10.

2.5". USA, 1950s. Plastic. $6-8.

Around The World. 3". USA, 1970s. $10-12.

"On Target" Cooler campaign. 4.25". USA, 1960s. Given to salesmen's wives as a reminder of prizes the salesmen could win during the "On Target" cooler/pre-mix placement campaign. Shown with original box. $45-50.

4.75". USA, 1980s. Coke Christmas set. Glass with metal tops. $15-18.

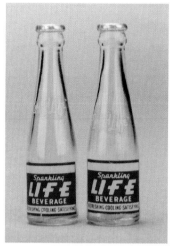

Sparkling Life Beverage, Milwaukee, Wisconsin. 4.25". USA, 1950s. $15-18.

Dr. Pepper. 6". USA, 1990s. Plastic. Munchkin Bottling Inc, Van Nuys, California. $6-8.

Far left:
7 Up and burger. 4". Sri Lanka, 1980s. Enesco. $15-18.

Left:
7 Up. 6.5". USA, 1994. Copyright Dr Pepper/7 Up Corp. Plastic. $6-8.

Below left:
Hires Root Beer. 5.25". USA, 1980s. Plastic. $10-12.

Royal Crown Cola. 5.75". USA, 1950s. ©1936 Nehi Corp. Glass with metal tops. $25-30.

7 Up. 4.25". USA, 1950s. Glass with metal tops. $15-18.

Left:
Canada Dry Ginger Ale. 4.5".
Canada, 1950s. Glass with metal
tops. $12-15.

Right:
Pepsi Christmas set. 6". USA,
1980s. $15-18.

Pepsi. 3.5-4.25". USA, 1940s. Glass with metal tops. Left set, $25-30.
Other sets, $15-18.

Pepsi 75th Anniversary edition.
Combination salt shaker and pepper
mill. 8.25". USA, 1970s. Wood. Shown
with original box. $18-20.

4". USA, 1950s. $15-18.

5.25". Left set,
USA. Right set,
France. 1970s.
$12-15.

173

Perrier. 3". France, 1990s. $100-110.

Pepsi. 6.25". USA, 1993. Plastic. License ©Pepsi Co. $6-8.

Right:
Perrier. 6.25". France, 1990s. $10-12.

Far right:
Virginia Dare. 5.75". USA, 1950s. Glass with metal tops. $18-20.

Below right:
Clearly Canadian Beverage Co. 5". USA, 1990s. $6-8.

Holly Beverages. 5.75". USA, 1950s. Glass with metal tops. $15-18.

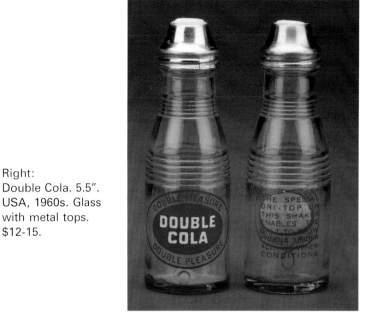

Right:
Double Cola. 5.5".
USA, 1960s. Glass
with metal tops.
$12-15.

A-Treat Ginger Ale,
Allentown, PA. 4". USA,
1950s. Glass with metal
tops. $10-12.

Cold Spot. 3.75". USA,
1950s. Plastic. $6-8.

Erie Beverages. 5.75". USA,
1950s. Glass with metal tops.
$15-18.

Double Cola. 4.5". USA, 1950s.
Glass with metal tops. $12-15.

Faygo. 5.75". Canada, 1950s.
Glass with plastic tops.
$18-20.

Left:
Golden Age
Beverages. 5.5".
USA, 1960s..
Glass with plastic
tops. $18-20.

Right:
Manhattan's
Ginger Ale and
White Soda,
Milwaukee,
Wisconsin. 4.25".
USA, 1950s.
Glass with metal
tops. $20-22.

Mission Beverages. 3.5". USA,
1950s. $12-15.

Nesbitt's of California. 3.5".
USA, 1950s. Glass with metal
tops. $12-15.

Crush. 3". Argentina,
1960s. Glass with metal
tops. $8-10.

Left:
Robinson Beverages.
5.75". USA, 1950s. Glass
with metal tops. $15-18.

Canada Dry Spur. 5.75".
USA, 1950s. Glass with
metal tops. $12-15.

Squirt. 4.5-5.75". USA, 1970s. Left set, $15-18.
Right set, $6-8.

Snow White. 5.5". Canada, 1960s.
Glass with plastic tops. $12-15.

Up-Town. 5.75". Canada,
1960s. Glass with plastic
tops. $15-18.

Vess Billion Bubble Beverages.
5.75". USA, 1960s. Glass with
plastic tops. $10-12.

BIBLIOGRAPHY

Conroy, Barbara J. *Restaurant China, Volume 1*. Paducah, KY: Collector Books, 1998.